TIME TO TALK

TRIGGER™
The mental health & wellbeing publisher

PRAISE FOR THIS BOOK

"The most important journey we must all take is the journey from our head to our heart and I honour Alex for his contribution in creating a safe space for men to do so. Thank you, Alex!"

Richie Bostock, The Breath Guy

"An invaluable primer for young men seeking a sense of identity and making sense of the world … *Time to Talk* is a timely and courageous offering."

Malcolm Stern, Co-founder of 'Alternatives', psychotherapist and author of *Slay Your Dragons with Compassion*

"A thoughtful, honest, helpful book on mental health, masculinity myths and the problem with 'manning up'. Alex has created a much needed space of community and compassion. A wonderful book on a topic that will help us all."

Emma Gannon, writer, broadcaster and bestselling author

"I long for a world in which all men are as curious, brave, and rigorous in the work of exploring and tending to their mental landscape, as Alex Holmes is. I believe reading this beautiful, thoughtful book will gently guide men who want to start on that journey."

Henry James Garrett, illustrator and author of *This Book Will Make You Kinder*

"A timely and truly important book that will no doubt help countless men"

Shahroo Izadi, Behavioural Change Specialist and author of *The Kindness Method*

"A really important book that every man should read. An extremely honest and vulnerable exploration of what it means to be a man, with some excellent advice and tips on how we can evolve to a more positive form of masculinity. I absolutely loved it."

Daniele Fiandaca, Co-founder of 'Utopia' and 'Token Man'

TIME TO TALK

How Men Feel About Love, Belonging and Connection

BY ALEX HOLMES

The mental health & wellbeing publisher

This edition published in 2023 by Trigger Publishing
An imprint of Shaw Callaghan Ltd

UK Office
The Stanley Building
7 Pancras Square
Kings Cross
London N1C 4AG

US Office
On Point Executive Center, Inc
3030 N Rocky Point Drive W
Suite 150
Tampa, FL 33607
www.triggerhub.org

First published by Welbeck Balance in 2021
Text Copyright © 2021 Alex Holmes

A CIP catalogue record for this book is available upon request from the British Library
ISBN: 978-1-83796-383-6
Ebook ISBN: 978-1-83796-384-3

Typeset by Westchester Publishing Services

ABOUT THE AUTHOR

Alex Holmes (Instagram @byalexholmes) is a mental health advocate, writer and podcaster. He uses compassion to help us reach our innermost selves, with the view to creating a safer world for men, women and children, through advocating for a positive, healthy and honest masculinity and mental health awareness. He hosts podcast *Time to Talk with Alex Holmes,* which focuses on ways to create a more compassionate world.

To all the men who could have loved
Had they been given the chance as boys
To grow into the best men
That they could have been.

FOREWORD

Alex Holmes is one of those people who makes you feel instantly at ease. In this unsafe world, he summons to mind E.M. Forster's line: "Only connect." The connections are not just between people, but between prose and passion, with the marvellous result that human love is celebrated.

Connection is the best possible solution for the inevitable struggles of being human. Reading these beautiful pages, we feel the connection with Alex and imagine that he feels it with us. In his calm, encouraging voice, Alex invites us to feel his acceptance of all that he is as he encourages us to develop a similar ease with ourselves.

Alex Holmes grasps the ambiguity of labels: "wife," "teenage boy," "Asian," "carpenter," "working class," "corporate executive." He presents the restrictions inherent to labels, causing individuals to be typecast by society. He reminds us that all human beings can recast themselves and choose who we want to become. He invites us to be who we want to be, rather than being confined to a label that is ill-suited.

His book is evidence of a life examined, of someone bravely bearing his soul and exploring his innermost self at the same time as urging you to do so. His own valiant work augments his credibility, and – the term is one of his favourites, essential to his values – "authenticity." He allows us to see his struggles and his triumphs; he could not be more intimate and trusting in the way that that he does so. His warmth, combined with his openness, becomes permissive to us. He sets an example not just of the *acceptability* of investigating ourselves more deeply and kindly and honestly, but of the *benefits*.

Psychotherapists know how incredibly daunting true psychological honesty can be. To see it on display, as it is in this book, is as encouraging to practitioners as it is to those in therapy. Alex makes the search pleasurable: "Come in," we imagine him saying, "And take a look around. There's nothing that needs to be hidden or denied." What a relief! And what a joy!

I have a vital personal connection to Alex Holmes. He contacted me at a dark and strange moment in my life. I was beginning to find my own voice, and felt uncertain about my next steps. The moment we met, I felt a kind of freedom to be myself. We were strangers coming together, but the immediate sense of calm understanding unburdened me. "Just be yourself," he seemed to say. "Whoever you are, what-ever you are, whether you're male, female, transgender, black, white, mixed, Asian, a teenager, a parent, an elderly person, single, married, asexual, unsure – the list goes on – just be *yourself*, and keep exploring what that means." And so we become unshackled.

Alex Holmes brings us to a place of hope. This is in large part because he acknowledges the sorrow and struggle of the battle to self-actualize. His bold recognition of pain enlarges the space for growth and possibility. Enlightenment can be a struggle, but its rewards more than merit the effort. And with this marvellous book, we not only enjoy personal gain and acquire unprecedented wisdom but, better still, we feel the beauty of all humanity.

Charlotte Fox Weber
Psychotherapist, writer and co-founder of Examined Life

CONTENTS

INTRODUCTION

In a 2019 episode of my *Time to Talk* podcast, Nick Bennett –
a friend of mine and founder of emotional fitness app Fika –
shared how he lost his best friend Ben to suicide in 2014.
Although he and Ben had known each other for years, he
realized that: 'We never really helped each other by talking.
We never really listened to each other properly. We just
basically met up, had fun and, quite frankly, got drunk.'

This simple observation of Nick's was a turning point for me
in deciding to write this book: a reminder of the urgent need
for as many voices as possible (whether expert or not) to join
the quest to get more people – men in particular – talking
about the things that matter in life:

- The things that make us tick – what makes or breaks us.
- How we're feeling, whether 'good' or 'bad'.
- Our worries. Our fears. Our vulnerabilities.
- How we feel about the big things in life – like love,
  belonging and connection.

- Ultimately, the ups and downs of our everyday reality, rather than any myths or polished versions of 'perfection' that we feel we should be living up to.

I wanted to get people talking with the aim of breaking the devastating cycle of so many men suffering in silence beneath what often *seem* like happy lives on the surface, yet feeling disconnected to the point that some feel life is no longer worth living.

This surface level of mates' banter that Nick mentioned, where certain 'norms' often tend to be accepted in terms of men not getting too 'deep' or serious about things, struck a chord with me. I've seen it in a lot of male friendships, including some of my own – old and new. And it can leave you feeling extremely lonely when things don't seem like they're going well in life.

Since recognizing this as a problem in my own life, I've worked hard to build deeper relationships where there is space for me to open up and be vulnerable about difficult issues, as well as to have a laugh. Stereotypical expressions like 'Man up', 'Be a man' and 'Don't be a girl' still hang around in the collective unconscious. It seems that many men suffer, albeit subconsciously, from underlying pressures about what 'makes a man a man' – including 'keeping schtum' about our emotions in case they lead to us being judged and rejected as not 'real men'.

Not that it isn't fun to have a laugh with friends, and joke about things, but it shouldn't be at the expense of talking about what's really going on in our lives and any serious issues that we need help with.

If we could all start talking and listening with more openness, honesty and vulnerability, as I have been learning to do while struggling with bouts of anxiety and depression since my final year at uni in 2014, I truly believe we can all start to feel more loved, less lonely and more connected – with a renewed sense that life really is worth living and loving.

A MENTAL HEALTH EPIDEMIC

According to recent figures from the World Health Organization (WHO), close to 800,000 people die worldwide due to suicide each year. That's a frightening one person every 40 seconds, and evidence indicates that for each person who died this way there may have been more than 20 others *attempting* suicide.

I am always shocked when I hear figures like these. Where have things gone so wrong?

WHO figures also reveal that the suicide rate is just over twice as high for men as for women; in 2017, the global rate for women was 6.3 deaths per 100,000, while for men, it was 13.9 per 100,000.

According to the UK's Office for National Statistics, there were 6,507 registered suicides in the UK in 2017, with a worrying three-quarters of these deaths being young men under 25. And, although suicide occurs across all age groups, it's now the second leading cause of death among 15–29-year-olds globally, with young Black youths not only potentially more at risk but also less likely, according to certain studies, of disclosing the concerns that lead to their suicidal thoughts due to the stigma that still surrounds mental health issues within Black communities in particular.

According to mentalhealth.org.uk, Black men are ten times more likely to suffer from a psychotic illness and four times more likely to be sectioned than white men. And members of marginalized groups, such as the BAME and LGBTQ communities, are generally believed to suffer mental health issues more from the weight of traditional masculine pressures than the cis-het normative community.

Data from the Samaritans has highlighted that many young people are self-harming as a way of trying to obtain relief from emotional distress and to express feelings that they find difficult to communicate in any other way.

In addition, mental health issues have been on the rise since the global COVID-19 pandemic ground the planet to a halt in 2020, bringing with it a combination of lack of social interaction, intense home situations during lockdown, rising financial pressures for many, and acute fears around health and wellness. A study from University College London revealed in July 2020 that 8,000 out of 44,000 people surveyed (almost a fifth!) reported thoughts of self-harm or suicide, and 42% had accessed mental health support services; a further 5% said they had harmed themselves at least once since the start of the UK's lockdown.

These statistics are devastating. And I'd like to think that they would be enough to get us all talking more openly about our mental and emotional health. But, unfortunately, while people generally go to a doctor to talk about a physical health problem, they often think that emotional and mental problems will get better of their own accord. Many people are also reluctant to talk openly or seek professional help due to a misplaced sense of shame and stigma. But we *must* talk if we want to start changing things.

As a young Black man who has experienced mental health struggles – firstly trying to cope on my own with my feelings of inadequacy and overwhelm, and, later, more openly, with the support of friends, family and therapy – I know we must break down the taboos and outdated myths around us men sharing our feelings and our worries.

THE PRESSURE TO 'MAN UP'

To be a young man – in my case, a young Black man – in today's world is to persistently hold your breath and hope you can come up for air sometime soon amid all the unspoken pressures of what we are, and aren't, expected to be by those around us. How we should 'fit' into society, and how we should be, both physically and emotionally: the notions of being ever-strong, resilient and unbreakable.

Generations of conditioning to not openly speak about our deeper emotional issues have caused many of us to develop a range of unhealthy habits of distrust and holding back. We traditionally don't share matters of the heart because we are expected to be rational and just get on with things.

Yet, no matter what gender, age, nationality, socio-cultural background or religion, we are all unique human beings with our own path to walk. So it only stands to reason that a one-size-fits-all, emotionally closed approach results in a deep sense of inauthenticity for many – a lack of self-acceptance, self-esteem, self-trust and self-love – and therefore a lack of feeling loved by others, a lack of sense of true belonging in life and a lack of meaningful connection.

This book is a response to this: an exploration of how men feel about what I have come to view in my research for this book as three of the cornerstones of emotional wellness: Love, Belonging and Connection.

Not that I can claim to speak for all men on these topics of course. But I hope that my insights in the pages that follow, gained from my own experiences and those of others – particularly those of the interviewees I have encountered over the past few years for my *Time to Talk* podcast – will at least encourage more open, honest conversations to be *started*.

WHO AM I TO WRITE ABOUT ALL THIS?

I'm Alex, a 28-year-old writer and podcaster of Afro-Caribbean descent, with a special interest in all things related to emotional and mental wellness. While I'm neither a mental health specialist nor a self-help expert, I am a firm believer that our mental health care is every bit as important as our physical health.

In 2018 I launched a podcast called 'What Matters', the name of which I changed to 'Time to Talk' in 2019 in order to highlight the core message I wanted to communicate. The aim of the podcast is to have wholehearted conversations with my guests about their lives in order to raise awareness around emotional and mental health – and therefore to create a safe space for people to talk, listen and reflect. This means interviewing people from many different backgrounds who have been through all sorts of mental health journeys – men in particular. And I'm immensely grateful to my guests for being so brave and open-hearted in sharing their stories and, in so doing, helping to break down the taboos around men talking about their emotions.

I have also been lucky enough to collaborate with mental health charities such as Shawmind, the Samaritans, and the British Red Cross.

Before becoming a full-time podcaster and writer in 2019, I spent several years working as a tabloid journalist in London. And before that, I spent my summers working as a youth mentor and one year as a teaching assistant in Reunion, a beautiful French-speaking island in the Indian Ocean. It was in Reunion that I first realized how much I loved working with young people, and the incredible power of conversation as a tool to help people develop and grow.

It was also in Reunion that, living in a predominantly Black community for the first time in my life, I realized just how much I had previously missed (without even knowing it at the time): the sense of belonging, connection and ease that came with *not* being part of a *minority* community. Not that I had felt actively alienated or unhappy as a Black boy growing up in West London. But, once back in England, I suddenly had a heightened sense of what being part of an ethnic minority meant, like being one of only five Black people out of about 40 or 50 studying French and Spanish (and over 100 studying languages), at Nottingham Trent University.

As a result I became much *more* aware of my Black heritage and the importance of learning about Black history, turning to writers such as Toni Morrison, James Baldwin, Malorie Blackman, Junot Diaz, Kei Miller, Langston Hughes and Maya Angelou for guidance – people whose works I have taken great comfort, strength and inspiration from ever since.

As I write this, I'm living at home with my parents and sister in London – one of the most expensive cities in the world. I am currently single and, in the spirit of us all wearing our heart on our sleeve more, I'm still exploring my *selfhood* and trying to get to grips with what it means for me, myself – a young Black man – to truly live a life full of love, belonging and connection.

MY JOURNEY TO THE POWER OF TALKING

I'm lucky enough to have grown up in a loving, warm-hearted family. I was a shy, sensitive, gentle and careful boy. I read a lot. I didn't like fighting or violence. And I cried easily.

Although I knew in my head that I was loved, looking back, I realize that I didn't feel that I was *truly* loved, that I *truly* belonged or that I was *truly* seen, heard and understood for who I really was, perhaps because I didn't live up to the unspoken expectations of what a boy (soon to be a man) really *should* be.

As mentioned, I cried easily and, therefore, often as a child. But one particular time stands out in my mind, when I was told by a distant female cousin at a family gathering to 'stop the tears' before a male relative saw me. From that day until my early twenties, when I first started experiencing the cumulative effects of bottling up my emotions in the form of bouts of anxiety and depression, I would only allow myself to cry when I thought it was deemed 'acceptable' to do so, funerals being a good example. Although I'd often feel upset by all sorts of painful events and interactions, I simply felt that I shouldn't – and therefore couldn't – show it on the outside.

As a result of this holding back, I started to feel disconnected from the people around me. And as I grew older and moved through school, then university, I grew anxious. I found and lost friends. I talked with lots of people but it was almost always playful banter rather than anything too deep or self-questioning.

I looked everywhere I could think of to try to find more of a sense of connection in my life. I threw myself into books, then church, then recreational drink and drugs, and even my writing, as a way to escape. But it wasn't until I was 23, several years after witnessing the London riots of 2011 (following the death of Mark Duggan, a local man who was shot dead by the police), and after entering the professional world as a news reporter, that I had a breakthrough – albeit induced by an initial break*down*.

The frustration and anger evident in the many young men involved in the London riots – which involved mass looting, arson and the unfortunate deaths of five people – was talked about by the media as a 'crisis in masculinity'. And something about this struck a deep chord with me as, while I couldn't identify with *their* specific rage, I, too, felt a lot of anger. An anger that was causing me deep pain and stopping me from feeling free. An anger that I didn't know what to do with and that hung over my head like a cloud of shame.

I remember hearing Diane Abbott MP talk in light of the London Riots about modern men feeling 'isolated and misdirected', saying that it seemed 'like the film *Fight Club* – where the first rule of being a man in modern Britain is that you're not allowed to talk about it'. And, again, this struck a chord: my anger was something that I didn't feel I could even *consider* talking to anyone about if I wanted to maintain any kind of status as a 'real man'.

Then, in 2015, I started working in a busy London newsroom – where the culture was very much fuelled by stereotypically masculine camaraderie and pressured deadlines. As I sat at my desk one day, I started to have what I now know were panic attacks – fast heartbeat, shortness of breath, racing thoughts and an inability to focus. This was accompanied by poor sleep at night and aching joints, which, on going to the doctor, turned out to be what he described as 'a worrying tendency at such a young age towards rheumatoid arthritis'.

I had been introduced to my job at one of the biggest papers in the UK via a diversity scheme, which I felt was looked upon by my colleagues at the time as an 'Ahh, that's why you're here!' As a result, I put myself under extreme pressure to 'prove myself' and 'succeed'.

I now know that I was suffering from serious imposter syndrome, allowing myself to be entirely engulfed by my worries about other people's *perceptions* of me – or rather what I *perceived* those might be. But at the time I didn't know quite what was happening and so began a search to get to the bottom of what was causing my physical symptoms.

I started to research and explore everything from journal writing and mindfulness to meditation and tai chi as a means of helping to manage my feelings. I read a lot and became familiar with the insights of a wide range of spiritual explorers, campaigners, wellness practitioners and teachers – from Russell Brand, Marianne Williamson, Shahroo Izadi and Natasha Devon to Richard Rohr, Eckhart Tolle and Thich Nhat Hanh, to name but a few.

Through all this, I came to the crucial realization that it was frustration, anger, emotional stress and unease that were at the root of my *physical* discomfort. It became clear that I needed to find a safe space to start opening up about the thoughts and feelings that were troubling me if I wanted to start to feel better.

I initially, nervously, confided in a few good friends and family members about how much I was struggling until, after a while, I felt comfortable enough to seek out a therapist to help me on my journey. I was lucky enough to find one who I clicked with, and I have now been seeing the same person (an integrative psychotherapist) for a few years on and off, depending on my finances.

With her help, I realized that I had been looking everywhere *outside* of myself for connection in my life but that it was now time to look *within* – and start an honest, inward conversation – in order for things to shift in my life.

And shift they did. This discovery of open, honest dialogue with both myself and others as a powerful means to clearing my head and regulating my emotions has been truly transformational for me. It is not something needy, embarrassing or shameful that only *weak* people need to do – which is how I now realize I had been subconsciously viewing it.

Being brave enough to overcome my fear of my personal thoughts and worries being dismissed, laughed at or rejected led to my anxiety and panic attacks largely subsiding and to me feeling lighter, better and healthier in myself.

RISING VOICES

Although there's still a long way to go when it comes to us men talking more openly about our feelings and our worries, thankfully there have been vast leaps forward in discussions about mental health over the past few years – particularly *men's* mental health.

It's been hugely inspiring to see more men, including high-profile ones, becoming vocal about where they're at with their emotions and challenging hypermasculine stereotypes – with a view to encouraging *other* men to open up and share their stories, too.

In 2017, British rapper Stormzy spoke about how his battle with depression encouraged him to create his first album, *Gang Signs and Prayer*, which was a 'realization of how fragile we are as humans … in the most beautiful way possible'. It wasn't until a good friend of his apparently confided in him about silent struggles with depression that he recognized many of the traits as being the same as his own; and he began to understand that the way men discuss mental health needed to change so that others would know that they weren't alone. He decided to talk about it publicly, saying, 'If there's anyone out there going through it, I think for them to see that I went through it, it would help. Because for a long time I used to think that soldiers don't go through that. You know? Like, strong people in life, the bravest, the most courageous people, they don't go through that, they just get on with it.'

American former swimmer and decorated Olympian Michael Phelps is another example of a celebrity figure stepping forward and talking openly, when in 2018 he admitted that, 'After years and years of just shoving every negative, bad feeling down to the point where, I mean, I just didn't even feel it anymore … I found myself in a spot where I didn't want to be alive anymore.' He credits his wife, Nicole, and therapy with getting him through, but highlights that it really wasn't easy. He told CNN: 'It's a dark, dark road sometimes, so you just want to make sure you are staying open. I'm very comfortable talking to my wife now … [and] with a therapist … but in the beginning, I wasn't.'

Ex-footballer Marvin Sordell also shared how he got to the point of trying to take his own life, as he felt unable to talk to anyone about just how low he was feeling – and how ashamed he felt about it. Rapper Professor Green opened up after his father took his own life in 2008, saying, 'We have to figure out a way that men can talk to one another and figure out how to make themselves feel better.' These are just a few of the high-profile men who have taken the brave decision to wear their heart on their sleeve with a view to helping others do the same.

Mental health charities such as CALM (Campaign Against Living Miserably) and the Shawmind Foundation (which has provided immense support with this book) have also been hugely instrumental in widening the conversation about mental wellbeing. As have writers such as Matt Haig, Stephen Fry, Derek Owusu, Natasha Devon and Jameela Jamil, who have notably all been open about their own challenges with mental health in their writing.

There have also been high-profile mental wellness campaigns such as 'Heads Together', spearheaded by the Duke and Duchess of Cambridge, and ITV's 'Get Britain Talking'. And TEDx talks such as Ben Hurst's 'Boys Won't Be Boys', Tony Porter's 'A Call To Men', Jake Tyler's 'Learning to Live with Depression' and Phillip J. Roundtree's 'Black Mental Health Matters' are all examples of people speaking about mental health and masculinity in ways that have not been seen before across the socio-economic and gender divides.

The mental health crisis that is engulfing society today, affecting boys and men in particular, means that more than ever before, it's Time to Talk.

SO, WHY ARE WE HERE?

AN EPIDEMIC OF LONELINESS

At this point in the 21st century, we are more 'connected' in some ways than we have ever been before. If we want to order food of almost any nationality, look up some important information, or speak to a friend or family member (whether upstairs, next door or in another country), we can do so at the press of a button.

Yet, despite all this *digital* connection, it seems that many of us are feeling more disconnected on an *emotional* level than ever before – not only from those around us, but also from our own sense of self.

An initiative called the Jo Cox Commission on Loneliness – set up in 2016 by the late Member of Parliament Jo Cox – undertook a study that resulted in loneliness being cited as a 'silent epidemic'. Sadly, it revealed that, of the people surveyed, 7% of men (more than 1 in 20) said they had no friends, and of those that did view themselves as having friends, 8% (nearly 1 in 10) said that none of them were actually *close* friends.

And during the COVID-19 pandemic and resulting lockdown in 2020, the BBC Loneliness Experiment – an online survey made up 46,000 people aged between 16 and 99 across 237 countries – revealed that men generally felt lonelier than women, with younger men feeling the loneliest, and the young men living in individualistic countries such as the US or UK feeling it the most.

Stats like these are deeply troubling, as we can't help but make a connection between this rising epidemic of loneliness among men and the rising epidemic of suicide and other forms of self-harm.

THE GROWING NEED FOR CONNECTION

As much of Western society has moved towards a more individualistic approach to life over the course of the last century, with less focus on extended families and communities, as well as on religion and spirituality, it seems that more and more people have started to feel lost and disconnected, as if missing a true part of themselves.

Traditional masculine pressures often mean men feel that they 'should' be able to cope with loneliness and sadness *alone*, and never actually acknowledge that they are struggling beneath the surface, exhausted from having to manage the load all by themselves.

What is really *needed* is for us men to take an honest look at how we're doing, come to terms with the fact that all is *not always* well:

- We *can* feel lonely.
- We *can* struggle.
- We *do* sometimes need companionship and intimacy, help and connection.

And THIS IS ALL OK.

This is not weak, or 'pathetic' or a burden on anyone.
This is simply part of being human.
We need people.
And, as such, while we might feel lonely at times,
WE ARE NOT ALONE.

Only once we establish this level of emotional *self*-awareness – having had a good honest 'talk' with ourselves about our situations – will we feel more grounded, more true to ourselves and more self-connected.

And only then will we start to break free from the chains of emotional disconnection that we have been socially conditioned to accept – the sense that we're not *allowed* to experience things like self-doubt, worry, fear and vulnerability.

And, from there, we will be able to start reaching out to, and connecting on a deeper level with, those around us again – sharing the stories of how we ended up here, exploring how this has been making us feel, letting our friends, family and trusted others *help* us in whatever way they can – so that we can all move forward feeling safer and more at ease with ourselves.

We all want to feel at home in ourselves, and so much of the process of reconnecting is simply about finding our own path towards that home. It is here that we can feel true love, belonging and connection again – but only once we realize that it is our fundamental right to be loved for who we are at our core (once all our masks of bravado have been dropped).

WHAT DOES EMOTIONAL DISCONNECTION FEEL LIKE?

Knowing what emotional disconnection can look and feel like in our lives is a crucial part of getting us to open up more about things – it allows us to first recognize the 'symptoms', if you like, of what might be shaking us to our very foundations.

I asked my followers on social media, a mix of men and women, to share how they have felt when in a state of *emotional* disconnection, and the most common answers were:

- Lonely (whether alone or with other people)
- Sad
- Stressed
- Overwhelmed
- Upset
- Anxious
- Discontented
- Ill-at-ease in own skin
- Angry with selves for feeling the way they do
- Uncomfortable acknowledging emotions, whether positive or negative (but especially negative)
- Unable to confront difficult or uncomfortable situations or truths
- Worried about opening up to anyone for fear of being laughed at or seen as weak
- Frustrated at not knowing how to express emotions
- Scared of being rejected by others if they knew how they were really feeling
- Inauthentic
- Unfulfilled
- Unseen and unheard
- Unvalued
- Empty (and not knowing how to fill the void)
- Stuck, with nowhere to turn
- Useless

- Worthless
- As if they are losing touch with reality
- Lacking purpose in life
- Lacking meaning in life
- Unloved, or knowing in their *head* that people around them love them, but not *feeling* this love
- Lacking a sense of true belonging in life

This list obviously isn't exhaustive; we could go on. But, while not a very uplifting read, hopefully it's a useful reference point.

Do any of these feelings resonate with you? If so, how and when have they shown up? What have you done about them? And what might you like to do about them moving forward?

Sometimes, emotional disconnection can also manifest itself physically, in the *body*, as it did for me in the form of panic attacks when I didn't get help with my worsening symptoms of anxiety. In my case, it also showed up in the form of body aches, inability to focus, insomnia and mood swings. Different people will experience different symptoms, from shallow breathing to headaches to bad skin to digestion problems, and more. So, always be on the lookout for any physical signs of emotional disconnection, too.

WHAT DOES EMOTIONAL CONNECTION FEEL LIKE?

In contrast to the 'symptoms' of emotional *disconnection* just discussed, what does emotional *connection* and emotional *wellness* look and feel like? Being able to recognize these feelings will help us either learn to value this in our current lives, or know what we would like to aim for in the future.

As before, I asked my followers for their thoughts, and their answers were:

- Confident
- Authentic
- Strong
- Resilient
- Contented
- At ease in own skin
- Emotionally safe
- Secure
- Happy
- Calm
- Accepting
- Self-Appreciative
- Grateful
- At peace with themselves
- Open-minded
- Flexible

- Sense of being valued
- Sense of purpose
- Sense of meaning
- Sense of feeling truly loved
- Deep sense of belonging
- Comfortable alone, but not feeling lonely
- Able to acknowledge own feelings and worries
- Happy to talk about those feelings and worries with trusted others
- Willing to share, help and support others in return

Like the previous list, this is not exhaustive, but hopefully it gives you a useful reference point – and maybe even an emotional checklist to see whether you feel any of these things in your life. And if you don't, whether you'd like to know how to start experiencing more of them.

It's important, of course, to remember that emotional wellness is an ongoing process. We are not going to be in all these positive states for the rest of our lives. There are going to be days when we don't feel so good or when unfortunate things happen. But if we can maintain a state of emotional connection beneath all else, we'll know that we always have the potential to reach these places even in our most difficult moments.

THE IMPACT OF DIGITAL CONNECTION

Our rising levels of screen-time these days – without real person-to-person interaction, eye contact, physical touch, and so on – could well be a contributing factor to many people's growing lack of emotional connection. All the more so when we take into account that the more time people spend screen-bound, the less time they tend to spend outdoors or exercising – both things that are good for our physical *and* mental wellbeing.

There's also an argument that we could be stuck in a vicious circle with this: the more time we spend online, the more emotionally disconnected we feel; and the more emotionally disconnected we feel, the more time we spend on quick-fix digital connection through social media, Zoom calls, interactive gaming, etc. to distract ourselves from the unhappiness.

Be aware of how much time you're spending online, following endless threads and perpetual swiping. Does it feel healthy and balanced? Or does it feel like a time drain, maybe even leaving you feeling somewhat empty and disconnected? Real socializing, and connecting, may seem like more of an effort, but it's so worth it in the end.

MOVING FROM HEADSPACE TO HEARTSPACE

So how do we start to shift from this state of emotional disconnection and unease to emotional connection and wellness?

One way to make the transition is to purposefully get *out* of the fixed thoughts and beliefs in our *heads*, which can get in our way and hold us back, and *turn* to the feelings and experiences in our *hearts*.

Traditionally men have often learned (whether consciously or not) that they 'should' be purely rational beings and keep their emotions locked up. But it doesn't look like this is serving many of us particularly well anymore.

We need to move out of a judgemental, self-critical headspace and into a kinder, more compassionate heartspace. No more locking things up in our heads and bolting the emotional door. Instead, we need to open the door between our head and our heart, in acknowledgement that each affects the other.

This shift to the heartspace will allow us to see ourselves through kinder, gentler eyes and start opening us up from the inside out – allowing us to drop the pointless bravado and engage more easily in meaningful conversation, and to accept rather than fight the flow of life.

KEY BENEFITS OF A HEADSPACE TO HEARTSPACE SHIFT

In making the shift from headspace to heartspace, my hope is that we can also shift:

- From Ignoring to Acknowledging
- From Being Closed to Being Open
- From Avoiding to Embracing
- From Expecting to Accepting
- From a Sense of Separation to a Sense of Being in it Together
- From Rigidity to Fluidity
- From Focusing on Thoughts to Focusing on Feelings

And ultimately ...

- From Fear to Love
- From Loneliness to Belonging
- From Disconnection to Connection

WHAT DO WE MEAN BY 'TALKING' – AND WHY?

As we've already discussed in the Introduction, it's traditionally tough for most men to talk more openly about themselves. So why is talking viewed as one of the best ways to start making the shift from headspace to heartspace? And what do I mean by 'talking'?

US psychologist Michael Cornwall says that talking 'connects our thoughts and feelings in ways that create space to share and express what is happening inside of us'. As such, talking is the invaluable vehicle that carries our thoughts and feelings out into the world.

When we say 'talk' here, it's important to understand that we mean *really* talk. Not superficial chat and banter, but talking about what is happening in our lives, our heads *and* our hearts. Talking about what is bothering us, possibly even keeping us awake at night. Telling our own stories, sharing our own perspectives and, in so doing, lightening the load on our own shoulders.

Talking like this is about learning how to express ourselves in real-time, without editing what we share. There can be a raw power in this that allows even the toughest person to reveal the innermost parts of themselves, and to release bottled-up feelings that they thought they had already handled.

WHO SHOULD WE TALK TO?

One important caveat here is that we need to be discerning, of course, about who we choose to trust and talk to. It is important that we feel completely safe, listened to and loved when we do pluck up the courage to share our stories.

But not everyone has the ability to open their hearts and listen open-heartedly and compassionately, without judgement and without wanting to provide quick-fix solutions. Not everyone has the headspace, heartspace or emotional maturity to be able to carry the burdens of another easily. And sometimes certain friends and family members are just too close to a situation, or their vision and expectations of you, to be of much true help.

So while we may be lucky enough to have existing friends, colleagues, family members or a romantic partner who we can trust to open up to about certain things, there will also be people who it's best *not* to open up to if you want to remain on good terms. Choosing who to talk to is a matter of trusting your instincts.

It's worth considering what talking options might be open to you, including some people who are less involved in the intricacies of your life than your most immediate loved ones. The good news is that there are lots of options on this front, including:

- Chat groups, including men's groups – either online or offline; these can give a helpful sense of togetherness and belonging
- New friends that you might meet through such groups – often people with shared experiences
- Helplines of charities specializing in mental health and suicide prevention – such as the Samaritans, MIND, CALM, Shawmind, Befrienders Worldwide, Crisis Text Line and numerous others – all of whom are instrumental in giving a listening ear to anyone in need (See page 225 for a list of such resources.)
- Professional help in the form of counselling or therapy; there are myriad options to choose from these days depending on your needs, so your doctor, a mental health charity or your local health advisor should be able to guide you in the right direction, depending on whether you would like in-person or distance sessions; one-to-one or group sessions; talking therapy or a more holistic approach like mindfulness or yoga therapy.

While all have their value, I'm a big advocate of the professional help option when possible, not only because of their specialist training, their relative subjectivity and the fact that you get to arrange regular times with them where you are their sole focus, but because there are some things that a therapist or counsellor is often able to access that just don't tend to come to the surface with family or friends.

Another thing that I've found exceptionally helpful when there's no-one around to speak to is keeping a journal. That way, any time I feel I could do with getting something off my mind, I write it down – it could be observations, insights, worries, obsessive thoughts or any of the other chatter in my head. And, while not a form of 'talking' as such, this is still a helpful dialogue with myself, which often allows me to let go of things and move forward feeling lighter.

The main thing I'm keen for you to take away from here is that there's no need to ever feel alone. You just need to decide upon who you want to talk to and how. We are all different and have different needs, so it's about figuring out what will work best for *you*.

THE POWER OF TALKING

There is immense power in being able to openly share our stories, our worries, our challenges and other difficult elements of our lives with trusted people. After all, no man is an island. And we can't possibly hope for fulfilling relationships as we move through life if we don't recognize the power of sharing. And through this book, I am sharing my own experiences and those of others in the hope of us all becoming more connected to, and compassionate about, one another's stories and truths.

THE BENEFITS OF TALKING

- Allows self-expression
- Enables authenticity
- Prevents unhealthy suppression
- Frees up both headspace and heartspace
- Prevents emotional build-up
- Reduces the weight of burdens you carry alone
- Involves trust
- Allows your truths to be heard
- Encourages you to confront things head-on
- Builds self-awareness
- Builds self-confidence
- Can provide distance and perspective from problems
- Encourages connection with others
- Reminds you that you are not alone

ABOUT THE BOOK

This book has been chiefly written as a reminder to men that it really *is* Time to Talk. It is also an exploration of how men feel about Love, Belonging and Connection – the three qualities that I have come to view as the cornerstones of emotional wellness. My hope is that if we can all be encouraged to think about, and talk about, these qualities more, we will be able to *feel* them more as well, which is what has happened in my own life.

CONVEYING THE THEMES OF LOVE, BELONGING AND CONNECTION

Interestingly though, when putting the book together, it didn't feel quite right to present three sections relating to the three cornerstones, as it appeared that such all-encompassing themes could easily start to cross over into one another.

My instincts led me instead towards presenting the book in chapters that would reflect more *specific* components of living a life of love, belonging and connection. So, after much consideration and delving into my personal core values, I decided on the following themes:

1. Self-Acceptance – with the main takeaway being 'It's OK to be Not OK'
2. Compassion and Self-Love – all about 'Learning to Just Be'
3. Bravery – all about 'Finding Strength in Vulnerability'
4. Health and Body Image – with the main takeaway being 'There's No Body Like Your Body'
5. Self-Worth – all about 'Redefining Success'
6. Love, Trust and Intimacy – all about 'Learning to Love Courageously'

NAVIGATING YOUR WAY THROUGH

Each chapter includes two main sub-sections that explore different key aspects of the positive theme in hand. For example, the chapter on Self-Acceptance explores 'Dealing with Our Inner Critic' and 'Dropping the Need for External Validation', and the chapter on Bravery explores 'Being Honest About How We Feel' and 'Seeing the Value of Asking for Help'.

The two sub-sections in each chapter follow a similar pattern:

- *My Point of Connection* – where I share my experiences of the theme in hand, ending on questions that I've asked myself about my experiences.

- *Another Perspective* – where you hear *another* person's real-life experiences of, and insights into, the theme in hand – everything from surviving PTSD, grieving friendships and tales of coming out, to navigating life after an emotionally abusive relationship, and reimagining personal successes.

- *On Reflection* – where I reflect on the stories we've just heard and explore various perspectives and viewpoints; this section usually also involves further real-life experiences.

- *Return to Connection* – where I come back to My Point of Connection story from the start of the section and consider, with hindsight, different ways I could have handled or viewed the events, taking into account the insights and fresh perspectives that have since emerged.

There are also uplifting 'Note to Self' statements scattered throughout the book. These are intended to be brief reminders of each section's main messages and can also be used as positive affirmations if desired.

I hope that the combination of stories, insights, reflections and 'Notes to Self' in each section will provide a useful springboard from which you can start your own conversations, and that you find some helpful insights among it all. Please feel free to read the text in whatever way best suits you – whether in the order it's presented or by dipping into specific sections that seem most relevant or take your fancy. Just do whatever works best for you.

REAL MAN MYTHS

There's one more layer to the book that I'd like to take a moment to explain before you get stuck into the main chapters, and that's the 'Real Man Myth' that you see related to each chapter:

1. **It's OK to be Not OK – Time to Talk About Self-Acceptance**
   Real Man Myth: 'Real Men Don't Doubt Themselves'

2. **Learning to Just Be – Time to Talk About Compassion and Self-Love**
   Real Man Myth: 'Real Men are Fearless Go-Getters'

3. **Finding Strength in Vulnerability – Time to Talk About Bravery**
   Real Man Myth: 'Real Men Don't Cry'

4. **There's No Body Like Your Body – Time to Talk About Health and Body Image**
   Real Man Myth: 'Real Men Have No Worries About Their Bodies'

5. **Redefining Success: Time to Talk About Self-Worth**
   Real Man Myth: 'Real Men Never Fail'

6. Learning to Love Courageously – Time to Talk About Love, Trust and Intimacy

Real Man Myth: 'Real Men are Lone Wolves'

I decided to add these after talking with a wide range of men about the six chapter themes, and realizing that there often seemed to be *common* pressures and expectations underlying each area in terms of what the guys felt that they 'should' or 'shouldn't' *be* or *do* to feel secure in their own perceived masculinity, i.e. to be considered a 'real man'.

Each 'Real Man Myth' represents a powerful and toxic, if often subconscious, voice in the heads of many men; a hypercritical voice that encourages us to remain stuck in cycles of outdated self-limitations that often bring feelings of inauthenticity, self-doubt, lack of self-worth and sometimes even self-loathing.

The myths may well, at first glance, look like ridiculously stereotypical and outdated ideas that, in theory, should no longer have a place in contemporary life. Yet, in my experience and the experience of many of the men I've spoken to about this, myths like this *do* live on for many as underlying expectations passed down from generation to generation about what it really means to be a 'man'.

Unfortunately the existence of such myths, even if we aren't consciously aware of their presence in our psyche,

often leads us to wear emotional 'masks' a lot of the time –
masks of bravado to hide our real selves from others out of
fear of rejection or not fitting in. And this can lead us down a
path of feeling inadequate, inauthentic, insecure and, you
guessed it, disconnected!

I really hope that this book will help men to become more
aware of any such underlying outdated pressures that are at
play in their own lives – and then recognize that it's time to
break free of these subconscious pressures once and for all.

It's time for a new conversation about what it means to be
a 'real man' – one in which masculinity is viewed in a more
open, well-rounded way. So, each of the six chapters ends
with a 'Real Man Reality' to counter the 'Real Man Myth'. For
example, by the end of Chapter 1 on Self-Acceptance, the
myth of 'Real Men don't doubt themselves' is transformed into
'Real Men experience self-doubt like anyone else'.

The more we can accept reality over myth, and get to know
ourselves and open up about all aspects of our lives, the more
comfortable and connected we will feel in our own skin.

PROVIDING A SAFE SPACE FOR YOU

My hope is that the pages that follow will offer you a safe
space to start exploring some of the issues that *you* and/or
your loved ones might encounter when it comes to the
all-important themes of Love, Belonging and Connection.

Let me be clear: I'm not claiming to say anything particularly new or groundbreaking. I'm simply keen to add my voice – and the insights I've gathered from my own experiences and interactions with others – to what I feel is a crucial conversation.

Although lots of people are now talking more openly about men's mental health, the messages still aren't always being truly heard, received or taken on board, which means many people are still suffering. It's therefore more important than ever to start or keep talking …

I have tried to write this book as openly and honestly as possible, which I have to admit has been tough as it's brought up lots of emotional memories, forced me to dig deep and made me feel pretty exposed and vulnerable at times.

The stories, discussions and insights come from the heart, with a desire to spark conversations about the core things that make us.

After all, no matter what our gender or background, none of us want to feel alone. And the good news is that we don't have to if we start simply talking more sincerely to one another, listening to one another and nurturing each other's mental and emotional health with trust and respect.

While this book is written from my perspective as a young Black man, please know that this doesn't mean it's a book *just* for young Black men, or even just for men. I'd love it to be read – and I hope enjoyed – by anyone who longs to experience more love, belonging and connection in their life, including the sisters, mothers, colleagues, partners and friends of men out there who may be feeling lonely at the moment – unable to open up as yet and get things off their chest …

I also offer it as a love letter to all those who have lost their lives but who *could* have felt a deep sense of love, belonging and connection had they only known how to drop the 'masks' of perfection that they felt they had to wear, and been able to step out of a place of fear and loneliness and open up their hearts to share and talk from a place of love and authenticity.

So, let's talk.

CHAPTER 1

IT'S OK TO BE NOT OK
Time to Talk About Self-Doubt and Self-Acceptance

From talking to my friends and peers, it seems pretty common for men to feel a pressure to be certain, confident and ever sure of themselves if they're to feel liked and be viewed as 'real men'. Yet, who among us, whatever our gender, hasn't experienced feelings of worry and self-doubt that can make us feel low or held back at times? It's certainly a feeling that I've experienced my own fair share of.

In this chapter, we will look at:

- Our inner critic – that persuasive negative internal voice that so often tries to take over our lives by telling us we're not good enough, strong enough, manly enough or whatever else. Is there anything we can do to prevent this voice from winning over and making us feel lonely and low?

- The opinions and projections of others. Why does it matter what others might think or say *about* us or *to* us? Does it really make sense to let others have such an impact on how we feel about ourselves?

Real Man Myth: 'Real Men Don't Doubt Themselves'

DEALING WITH OUR INNER CRITIC

Whether we're aware of it or not, we're all impacted by our inner critic at times – the internal voice that causes us to question ourselves, our abilities, our decisions … A friend of mine sat listening to me once, then said, 'We need to work on your negative self-talk.' I hadn't realized how much of it there was, but it was true that it was kind of controlling me. That's why it's so important that we become more aware of it and explore ways to deal with it.

MY POINT OF CONNECTION

I recently went through a period of my sleep being badly disturbed by an influx of worries that I couldn't shake: 'When will I earn enough money to live independently? Why have I never had any luck in love? I don't look anything as good as other guys; I need to get to the gym! Why the hell am I awake at this time anyway? How am I going to get up for work in the morning?'

My inner critic was on overdrive, jumping from one thing to another, like a monkey leaping restlessly from branch to branch. And the more I battled the thoughts in pursuit of the sleep that wouldn't come, the more frustrated and annoyed I felt at myself.

The self-criticism would follow me into the daytime too, sowing seeds of doubt about whether I could achieve my goals for the day, and making me compare myself negatively to colleagues and friends. It even followed me when I went for my daily 'me time' walk to the canal near my home, where I like to connect with nature by watching the canal boats on the still water.

Thankfully I've started sleeping better again now, but the incessant voice of my inner critic is often still with me during the day. And I find myself wishing desperately for its hyperactive 'monkey mind' thoughts to leave me alone. They're a reminder that I often don't feel like the self-assured man I'd like to be and that I feel I 'should' be by this stage in life.

At times all the thoughts of inadequacy and insecurity become overwhelming, reducing me to tears. And, on my worst days, they can even bring on thoughts that it might be better if I weren't here at all anymore.

I feel bad for letting the negative thoughts get the better of me in the first place, when I know how lucky I am in so many ways to have so many good things in my life.

During such times, I can't help but ask myself questions like:

- *As a grown man, am I supposed to have so many negative thoughts about myself?*
- *Aren't I supposed to be self-assured and confident by now?*
- *Why do other men seem to have it all together, and I don't?*
- *The noise in my head is so overwhelming: why do I let it get to me so much?*
- *Are there ways I can stop feeling so unsure of myself and start feeling calmer and more confident?*

As I mulled over questions like this in preparation to write this book, an example from an inspiring woman I once heard give a talk about overcoming fear and self-doubt sprang to mind.

ANOTHER PERSPECTIVE

In 2016, a mentor of mine kindly organized a talk by a world-class rower for a group of Black men, as part of a series of empowerment conversations. During the talk, the woman told us about her experiences rowing across the Atlantic Ocean with her team. She painted a vivid picture of the trials they had faced, including how the boat had overturned among the violent waves and unforgiving winds, and how they had to salvage the situation.

I was in awe at the mere idea of having to face such a life-threatening situation. She explained, however, that the trick to overcoming the obstacles, achieving the goal in hand – and to surviving! – was to *embrace* the challenges, rather than in any way resist or shy away from them. At the end of the day, the waves and the winds were real and couldn't be denied, so they simply had to be dealt with.

Was she tired or frightened at times? With moments of great worry and doubt? Of course. But she knew that that was OK! It was a tiring, frightening and, at times, worrying situation. But the key was to acknowledge and accept the negative feelings and let them pass on by rather than allowing them to fester, grow, get in the way and define the situation.

She explained that the thoughts that she *chose* to keep in the foreground of her mind were therefore crucial, and these were: that she had trained for this, that she *could* do this and that she *was* going to get the boat back on track and complete the challenge. By neither frantically resisting nor dwelling on the doubts, worries and fears, and instead just letting them pass by and focusing on the positive, she could find the much-needed calm among the chaos to keep going, survive and thrive!

ON REFLECTION

Finding Still Water Beneath the Waves

I was deeply grateful to this athlete for her talk, as, coupled with various books I was reading and the guidance I was getting in therapy, it gave me a new perspective on my constant mind chatter of niggling self-doubts. It made me realize that, although it may look on the outside like everyone else is doing great all the time, *no-one* feels entirely sure of themselves *all* the time – not even a world-class rower like this. *Everyone* experiences elements of self-doubt. It's part of the human experience, no matter how fit and strong we are, no matter how sensible or level-headed we are, and no matter what gender we are. And that's OK! So there's simply no need to beat ourselves up about it!

I gradually came to the realization that having a lot of mind chatter and 'head noise' is therefore in no way a sign of weakness, failure, an inability to cope or a symptom of not being 'manly' enough, which is what I had really been feeling subconsciously.

Instead, mind chatter is simply what goes on in *most* people's heads; experts estimate that we have between 60,000 and 80,000 thoughts per day; that's an average of 2,500–3,000 per hour! Unfortunately, however, this often isn't talked about among men in particular. And if we don't express or talk about certain thoughts and worries, it can make them fester and magnify inside of us and they end up seeming so much bigger than they really are.

The more I thought about this, the more I realized how important it is to see that, while it's healthy to acknowledge and accept any negative thoughts and feelings that come up as part of your regular 'mind chatter', there's no need to get bogged down in them. Instead, it's good to learn to try to just *watch* the thoughts come and go as the rower did, like waves rising and falling on water – knowing that although turbulence may be inevitable at times, still waters always *do* lie beneath if we can just trust in this.

I was curious about other people's perspective of wanting to be able to pay less attention to the nagging voice of their inner critic – in order to be more self-accepting and contented – so I talked to a few friends and colleagues about it.

Trust Over Fear

A life coach and podcaster friend called Alex talked with me about the paralysing level of self-doubt that he experienced when he first decided to go into coaching. 'I was drowned in self-doubt. I didn't know whether I would be able to help anyone. I was worried about charging money for my services; worried about looking like I was just trying to make money from vulnerable people; worried about how to go about finding clients; worried about how people would perceive me as a new coach. I was worried about *everything*.'

But, after a period of letting this hold him back and feeling hugely frustrated, he realized that the only way for him to get past this negative mind chatter seemed to be to take a step back from all the 'noise' of the worry and to make an empowering choice to trust in the process. So, instead of chasing every worry at 100mph, he made a conscious effort to slow down, let the self-doubts float on by, focused on really connecting with each person he met and just went from there. After about a year of committing to this approach, he was amazed to realize just how much less of a hold his negative inner critic had on his life, how much happier he felt as a result, and how well he started doing as a coach.

Acceptance Over Comparison
My friend Alan, a 36-year-old from London, used to regularly self-harm. I would meet him for a coffee and his arms would be all scarred. When I broached the subject, a look of shame would come across his face.

He felt he was letting people down because he wasn't where he felt he should be *as a man;* he was still living at home, working in a job he didn't want to be in, and he hadn't found any guiding light or passion in life. When I asked him,

'What are the things you love about yourself?', he simply answered, 'I don't.' And it followed that he didn't feel that anyone *else* could really love and accept him either. His inner critic – in this case one formed by having been heavily criticized and emotionally neglected as he grew up – was doing quite some job at making him feel worthless.

This friend and I fell out of regular contact after a while but when I next saw him about a year later, he was in a good space. He had moved jobs, was working on more enjoyable projects, and was much happier in himself. He admitted that he still struggled at times but that he now knew this was *OK* – and 'normal' for many – so there was no need to punish himself for it. The key for him had been learning to accept where he was in life instead of obsessively worrying about it, comparing himself to other guys or beating himself up about it. This willingness to just *accept* himself, wild thoughts and all, had created space – and energy! – for him to start to make the changes he wanted to make in life.

Note to Self

How I navigate the world starts with how I think about and speak to myself today, tomorrow and the next day.
It is up to me what thoughts I allow to define me –
and set me free.

A RETURN TO CONNECTION

Seeking Clarity: We are Not Our Thoughts

Going back to My Point of Connection story on page 44 – where I allowed my negative thoughts to impact the way I saw myself in the world and ultimately stop me from stepping into the person I wanted to be ...

If I were to re-run this scenario through a lens of more self-acceptance, I could allow myself to hear and *acknowledge* the voice of my 'monkey mind' inner critic both during the night and the next day without surrendering to it.

And thinking back to the kind of questions I was asking myself at that time:

- *As a grown man, am I supposed to have so many negative thoughts about myself?*
- *Aren't I supposed to be self-assured and confident by now?*
- *Why do other men seem to have it all together, and I don't?*
- *The noise in my head is so overwhelming: why do I let it get to me so much?*
- *Are there ways I can stop feeling so unsure of myself and start feeling calmer and more confident?*

… I now realize that:

- It's absolutely *OK* to have negative thoughts and self-doubts, and to not feel entirely OK all the time; it happens to us *all* at times.
- Just because worries and self-doubt raise their head now and again, it doesn't mean I can't be a generally confident, self-assured person. Sure, in an ideal world it would be fantastic if we could all live life feeling accepting of ourselves *all* of the time! But we are emotional beings, so it's part of the richness of life to have ups and downs.
- Although it might *look* like everyone around me is sorted and doing brilliantly, we all have our own worries beneath the surface, so we are not alone!
- It can definitely feel like there's a lot to deal with at times in life. But it's important to remember I can make a conscious choice at any time to take a step back from all the noise in my head to gain more of a sense of perspective and peace.
- Thoughts are just thoughts – they will pass if I don't let myself get bogged down by them.

- As such, I don't need to keep listening to the worries and doubts.
- I don't need to buy into them, feed them or allow them to define me.

- I can instead make the choice to just *watch* them and let them pass by.

Accepting ourselves in this way – worries and all – is the first step to reclaiming our own sense of connection, power and freedom in the world.

Not that this shift from self-doubt and self-criticism to self-acceptance is an easy one to make in the long term, of course. I all too often become a slave to my inner critic again, believing what it tells me I am in the moment.

In a 2013 *New York Times* article, Professor of Communications at University of Connecticut–Stamford, Clifford Nass (also co-author of *The Man Who Lied to His Laptop: What We Can Learn About Ourselves From Our Machines*), was cited as having said: 'Negative emotions generally require more thinking, and the information is processed more thoroughly than positive ones.' This makes sense of why we tend to find ourselves obsessing over negative thoughts and emotions much more frequently and lengthily than over positive ones. But does this serve us to be the people we want to be – living lives full of love, belonging and connection with both ourselves and others? Of course not!

My hope is that the stories and perspectives I've shared here about the negative thoughts we *all* sometimes experience might help us start being less harsh on ourselves, and more accepting. It happens to all of us. We all have our moments.

Another common way in which we often limit our own potential for self-acceptance is by getting bogged down in what *other* people think and say about us, whether friends, family, colleagues or strangers.

DROPPING THE NEED FOR EXTERNAL VALIDATION

As a writer and interviewer, words are important to me, but how much should we, and do we, let the words and opinions of others affect the way we view ourselves and plant seeds of self-doubt in our heads? The old adage 'Sticks and stones will break my bones but words will never hurt me' is often suggested as a retort when you're a child in the playground, but does it really hold true when it feels like words can carry so much power? It's time to talk about just how much they *can* hurt us, just how much influence they can have over our capacity to love and accept ourselves, and what we can start to do about this.

MY POINT OF CONNECTION
On 13th May 2018, I received a direct message on Twitter, letting me know that I should 'be careful'. Baffled, I went to my timeline and found an anonymously created 'List of Abusers in the Creative Industry' posted there, which included

my name. Next to each name on the list was a brief description of the claim. Beside mine, it said 'harassment and violently homophobic'.

My initial reaction was to laugh at the ludicrousness of the claims. Homophobia and harassment? That sure as hell wasn't me. But as I began to think about who would be malicious enough to create such a list – and why – a mixture of emotions started to course through me, from disbelief, hurt and disappointment to self-doubt, shame and anger.

I couldn't get my head around the fact that someone would do this to a well-meaning person like myself, especially in such an anonymous, public bombshell way. It felt deeply unfair. My loved ones and I knew that the claims were untrue, of course. And some people questioned the basis of the claim. But that didn't stop a lot of others getting caught up in the drama of it all. I received all sorts of abusive messages. Online 'friends' started to block me. People began to gossip about me on private accounts. A lot of people I had come to view as friends turned their backs on me in the face of all the toxic 'noise'.

I knew deep down that I shouldn't let the misguided opinions of others bother me. But they did, and the whole experience really impacted on me. I got so much abuse over the next few days that I deactivated Twitter, became frightened to go to events and hid away at home (other than going to work) for as long as I could. I started to worry that, given that a lot of people no longer seemed to believe that I was a good-natured, open-hearted person, maybe I wasn't these things. I became a shell of myself, and the level of disconnection I felt was crippling.

In the moment, I felt like the online community I had been working so hard to become a part of had turned its back on me. I fell into an abyss – no longer knowing who or what to trust, my own thoughts included. And it took me over a year and a half to rebuild my self-belief with the help of my true friends, as well as my therapist, who encouraged me to work through all the difficult emotions around the trauma of the social media attack.

During this time, I couldn't help but ask myself questions like:

- Were the things that were being said about me in some way true?
- Was I not the good-hearted, open-minded person I thought I was?
- Were the thoughts and words of others really a reflection of who I am as a person?
- Why am I letting what others say drag me down so much?
- How can I move forward from this and not be as affected by other people's opinions of me?

ANOTHER PERSPECTIVE

In my quest to find answers to the questions above, I started talking to other men about the impact that the things said by the people around us can have on how we feel about ourselves. As part of this, I found a friend in 31-year-old Josh Rivers, the host of popular podcast 'Busy Being Black', which he set up in 2018 to encourage queer Black people to lead their fullest lives.

In 2017, Josh went through the terrible experience of prejudiced tweets from his youth being dug up and used against him; things that he would simply never dream of writing now and that in no way represent the *true* essence of his character, but that were an unfortunate product of him growing up online.

The unearthing of these tweets lost Josh his landmark position as the first Black editor of *Gay Times* magazine. And, when I interviewed him for my podcast, he explained how the combination of the online abuse, the public humiliation, the loss of his job and the all-encompassing notion of others now seeing him through such a negative lens completely shattered his sense of self-worth, causing him to withdraw from online life for quite some time.

While he felt terrible that he had ever written such tweets in the first place and had to deal with the emotions surrounding his ignorance in his earlier years, he also had to find a space from which to deal with the emotional damage that the comments were *now* causing him. 'Social media consists of apps on phones. It is not "real", he said. 'So how can we allow it to have such an impact on our lives?' Yet impact his life it *did*, in that he, like me, started to worry not only about how others would be towards him but also to doubt the very fabric of his own character.

While Josh didn't talk to a therapist about his situation straightaway, he did, in the end, decide it would be useful. Through therapy he came to realize that the only way for him to heal and move forward in a positive way was to confront the insecurities that the situation had brought to the surface. He had to forgive not only the people who had brought the tweets to light and sent him the subsequent abuse, but also forgive *himself* – both for writing the tweets in the first place and for how much he had been letting all the abuse get to him. 'I think what I've learned about myself in this past year', he said, 'is that I have to take the act of forgiveness much more seriously. I don't think I forgive people easily anyway, but I really don't forgive myself. Sometimes I see myself doing something and think, "You're punishing yourself, self-sabotaging yourself. You don't think you deserve happiness, success or love …". But, in reality, we *all* deserve these things, right? So why am I not giving myself permission to fully experience them?'

Ultimately, his negative online experience taught him a lot about the importance of getting to know himself better and accept himself more, and is, in the end, what led him to start his amazing 'Busy Being Black' podcast – a safe, supportive space for queer Black people, like himself, to be their authentic selves, share their stories and recognize their *own* right to love, belonging, connection and happiness.

ON REFLECTION

Moving Away from Shame

When you encounter a negative experience online in the way that Josh and I did, it can leave you thinking more negatively about yourself than you ever thought was possible.

At the time of writing this, the devastating suicide of British television presenter Caroline Flack has been tied to internet trolling and media intrusion into her personal life. And, unfortunately, this is only one of many such instances. Black footballers in the UK, such as Raheem Sterling, Danny Rose and former player Ian Wright, are among the many who have recently experienced a slew of online racist abuse. And when US rapper Lil Nas X came out as gay in 2019, after considering 'taking his sexuality to the grave', he got a huge amount of abuse (as well as support), with people tweeting things like *'That's it. I'm not ever listening to @LilNasX cos I don't wanna turn gay …'* Although he bounced back in the end, the level of negative comments caused him to initially tweet that he didn't want to make music anymore.

As we know, abuse can, unfortunately, come in many forms, both on- and offline: racism, sexism, homophobia, body shaming, 'slut-shaming', or general bullying. The recent #BeKind movement, which encourages more positive, thoughtful and compassionate interaction, is therefore a timely and much-needed one.

There's certainly a conversation to be had here about why the kind of online toxicity that so many experience is so rife; perhaps the fact that people are doing this from behind the safety of screens, may partially be why they are more willing to make all sorts of claims that they wouldn't necessarily say face to face.

However, I want to focus here on *why* we let the comments and opinions of others – whether online or offline, negative or positive – become so important to us and impact our sense of self so much in the first place, causing so much stress, *distress* and self-doubt.

We Are Not What Others Say About Us

I have realized since my trolling experience that, while deeply traumatic for me at the time, ultimately, it offered me a valuable chance to look at my own patterns of behaviour, accept them and learn from them. A chance to look at what

I really think about *myself*, rather than what others think of me, which I realized I had been focusing on up until that point.

I started to understand that the reason my sense of self-worth had been so entirely upturned by the online abuse was that I was entirely reliant on the *external* views of *others* – and them accepting, approving and 'liking' me – to give me a sense of love, belonging and connection, instead of learning to accept and like myself!

My foundations were shaken to the core because I hadn't spent time building my *own* strong foundations in the first place. I had been living as if the opinions of others were what defined me, instead of my sense of self-worth being in my own hands.

I realized that we have to be brave enough to push past perceptions of what we feel we 'should' be as men, and let go of the comments and judgements that others are constantly making around us in order to get to know and accept our true authentic selves, no matter what others may think or say about this.

Countering Negativity with Positivity

When I talked to 26-year-old photographer Francis about self-doubt created by the reactions of others, his take was that, as a creative Black man, it was something he was 'constantly battling'.

'It's not about pushing it out of my brain; it's more about understanding that it's there, reminding myself that it's OK that I feel this [a certain] way about it and then taking care of it.' For him, he says this is about taking time to figure out what thought pattern is causing the self-doubt, asking where the opportunity to grow is in this, and then replacing the negative narratives about himself with more positive ones.

'I went to an event led by Black male entrepreneurs and heard the saying, "As a man thinketh, so is he", and it stuck with me what a real effect our thoughts have on our bodies and actions. So now, when something negative happens to me [or is said to me], and I start to feel uncomfortable in my masculinity, I bring to mind that quote and give myself positive affirmations to help me through it.'

As a result, Francis feels confident in saying: 'I'm now in a place where it's relatively hard for self-doubt ... to completely rule my mental dominion. I have a strong foundation in terms of where I am as a man, what is important to me and what kind of person I want to be.'

Developing Strong Core Values

I also talked about self-doubt to Kai, a 36-year-old youth worker and campaigner who works with Black boys to challenge their inherited notions of masculinity. We talked about having both been raised in a culture that we felt was a lot about 'de-sissifying boys', and how much this had inhibited our self-expression and limited our ability to accept many aspects of ourselves.

He shared that he had 'always been naturally drawn to colourful things', but that the desire to express this in what he wore felt like an 'internal battle for a long time', as it caused the 'ugly troll' of self-doubt to pop up in his mind due to his worry about how others would perceive it. But the more Kai worked on building what he describes as 'the foundations of [his] value and self-esteem', and the more he reminded himself that, no matter what he does or wears, and no matter 'whether people laugh at me or think [what I'm wearing] is whack, I am still someone of value and that cannot be changed.' Kai said it was a big thing for him to 'learn to detach my sense of self-worth from *external* validations and accolades, and to instead base it on what I feel and believe about *myself*.' Once he learned this, he became immeasurably less susceptible to the negative impact of the opinions of others, and more able to fully embrace himself in a way that transformed his perception about his place in the world.

Note to Self
To accept myself is to remember who I was
Before I was conscious of the way
People thought of me.

A RETURN TO CONNECTION

Being Kind to Ourselves – and Others

Coming back to the online experience that Josh and I had, we both realized through talking to others that the first steps towards us shedding our self-doubt and moving forward more positively were forgiving ourselves for the mistakes we had made in the past; then forgiving the people who had attacked us for this, in the knowledge that their lashing out was likely at least in part an expression of their *own* pain; and, finally, not beating ourselves up for allowing the negative online interactions to *uproot* us to the extent that they did.

We both needed to acknowledge that it was OK to find such negative bombardment difficult, as being 'attacked', even in the online sphere, has the potential to send us into the natural human survival response of 'fight or flight'. The trick is not to let yourself fall into either of these options – getting defensive and striking out in anger *or* hiding away – in the long term. But, instead, to use the experiences as a chance to check in with whether we are living and acting in line with our *own* values in life. Or, in my case, to explore what my core values in life really were in the first place.

Building Firmer Foundations

My therapist encouraged me to spend time on exploring my core values, including working out the difference between my goals and my core values. She asked me to imagine

I was driving a car to a particular destination – my 'goal'. We can have many goals in life; we might want to own a house, have a big family, run several businesses, travel the world by a certain age … However, the irony, she explained, is that sometimes when we reach these 'goals', we still don't feel fulfilled. So, maybe it's not the destination that's important, but *how* we get there – what we see and do along the way, how we interact with others, etc. – based on our core values.

I realized through this that I had been largely focusing on superficial goals, such as to be popular and to be seen as an influencer. This had led to me feeling devastated by the idea of others thinking badly of me, rather than focusing on *how* I wanted to be along the *way*, such as loving and respectful to both myself and others, which would allow me to travel towards my goals from a more authentic, grounded, aligned and self-accepting place.

This realization was a game-changer for me, and my core values have been my anchors in life ever since; they are the things I can return to in order to feel grounded and safe when things get tough. When I return to events in my life and see that the decisions I've made, words I've said or actions I've taken are in line with them, I know I have nothing to feel shame or anger about, no matter what others may be saying. And with these negative emotions out of the way, I've been able to enjoy once more a sense of trust and confidence in myself as a fundamentally *good* person, with *good* intentions.

Taking it to 'Real Life'

Of course, it's not just in connection with online scenarios that it serves us to stop doubting ourselves based on what others say. 'Real-life' scenarios of bullying, abuse (whether conscious or not on the part of the abuser), and even just lots of small, thoughtless or insensitive comments can all take their toll on our mental health if we're not careful. So it's important to look out for these things in our lives too, and be willing to look at them and talk about them, rather than letting their toxicity fester.

If, for example, something that a friend, colleague or partner says upsets us in some way and we choose *not* to address it (which can often feel easier in the short term), the likelihood is that, in the longer term, any negative 'stories' it causes within our own heads – whether that be that the person hates us, that they think we're awful people or that they don't love or care for us – will grow and make us feel terrible. If, on the other hand, we can speak honestly about the issue, things would at least be out in the open, with a chance of being resolved and moving forward.

What We Feed Our Minds Becomes Us

It's important to remember that we have the power, at least to some extent, over what we 'feed' our minds in the first place – just as we have power over what we feed our bodies.

If we are constantly on social media consuming information that is negative, or if we're reading trashy magazines, watching violent TV programmes, and spending time with people who talk badly of us or others, it's like eating junk food and sweets all day long – it *will* have a negative effect on us after a while. It's therefore up to us to create boundaries for what we 'consume', and to put in place strategies that we can use for when we *do* encounter things that we know are bad for us.

Just like we might choose to be kind to ourselves by going for a long walk or by heading to the gym to work off recent excessive eating, we can also choose to do something positive if we find ourselves suffering as a result of things people have said about us.

Whether it's returning to our core values in our head or on paper, or writing down how we feel to get it out of our system, or talking to trusted friends or family, or sharing our experiences with a therapist, there is always a way through that can get us grounded and back to who we are.

Seeking Clarity: Self-Acceptance is an Inside Job

Returning then to the questions that I found myself posing in my own head after my experience of online abuse:

- *Were the things that were being said about me in some way true?*
- *Was I not the good-hearted, open-minded person I thought I was?*
- *Were the thoughts and words of others really a reflection of who I am as a person?*
- *Why am I letting what others say drag me down so much?*
- *How can I move forward from this and not be as affected by other people's opinions of me?*

… I now feel comfortable in the knowledge that:

- While the things that people said about me online were, in my eyes, untrue and hurtful, they allowed me to look back and reconsider my social media interactions when I was younger, and learn from them.
- Despite what some others may think of me from the outside looking in as a result of the negative online comments, nothing has changed from the inside looking out. I am still the

same good-hearted person, doing my best to live by a set of positive, open-minded life values.

- The thoughts and words of others are just *their* thoughts and words, formed in *their* minds via *their* own particular lens. As such, they are not ours to control and they rarely serve as any kind of true reflection of the type of people we are.

- We often focus so much on getting positive external approval – from what *others* think and say – that we can lose sight of looking inwards. It is important to check that we are happy with our *own* core beliefs and whether we are living our life around them.

- When we get to know and feel attuned to our *own* values in life, our foundations will be unshakeable, no matter what others may say or do.

And with the support of solid foundations, we can drop any masks we have been wearing to try to live up to the myth that 'Real Men don't doubt themselves', and step into the authenticity of who we really are. Only then can we open up to accepting, liking and loving ourselves again, or, for some, for the first time in our lives.

REAL MEN – THE REALITY

It's Time to Drop the Myth That:
Real Men don't doubt themselves.

It's Time to Remember That:
Real Men experience self-doubt like anyone else. The more we can accept self-doubt, get to know ourselves and open up about all aspects of our lives, the more comfortable and connected we will feel in our own skin.

CHAPTER 2

LEARNING JUST TO BE
Time to Talk About
Compassion and Self-Love

From a young age, guys are often given the idea that it's their role to *do* things and to *fix* things – to be action men, tough men, superheroes, go-getters – whether by being *physically* active through sport; super practical by fixing broken-down cars and putting up shelves; or fearless and dynamic by making the first move in romantic relationships.

But what space do these kinds of expectations leave for us to just *be*, rather than constantly *doing*? Especially if we don't fit these traditional notions of masculinity?

Isn't it time we created more space for us all to just *be* and to *love* our *authentic* selves, rather than trying to *force* ourselves into a 'real man'-shaped mould that we don't feel comfortable in? Wouldn't we feel happier if we could show ourselves compassion and self-love rather than the disdain and self-loathing that I know I and many of my male friends have experienced at times?

In this chapter we will look at:

- The power of valuing ourselves as human *beings*, rather than human *doings*. Wouldn't it feel good if we could stop trying to 'fix' who we are and just enjoy *being*, whatever that looks like for each of us as individuals?
- The importance of getting to know and love our authentic selves so that we can drop any masks we've been wearing to try to meet *other* people's notions of masculinity. Wouldn't it be great if we could all treat ourselves and one another with compassion and love for who we really are?

Real Man Myth: 'Real Men are Fearless Go-Getters'

RECOGNIZING THAT WE ARE NOT BROKEN

In my experience, the pressure on men to *do* certain things, *act* in certain ways and *fix* everything can leave many of us feeling like *we* are in some way broken and in need of *fixing*! So, I'm keen to look more closely at what we can do about this sense of inadequacy that so many experience.

MY POINT OF CONNECTION

I have a strong memory of playing basketball when I was 16 and one of the guys telling me in no uncertain terms to 'man up'.

I can still remember the way he looked at me, before going on to say that I needed to 'fix up', and that I should be 'manlier', instead of 'flimsy like a woman'. I was playing centre, so I guess he felt that I wasn't showing quite the strength he deemed appropriate to defend the hoop from point-guards or the aggression he felt was needed to score on close shots and rebound.

I had a similar experience on the basketball court when I was 18 and my school PE teacher said, 'We tried to fix you into being a jock, but you didn't bite, did you?' And I had another similar experience with a personal trainer who said I needed to be 'less of a woman' when it came to weight training, as he didn't feel I was being as focused or aggressive as I could be.

I remember my parents spending quite a bit of time trying to show me things like how to walk 'more like a man' – with my feet outward rather than inward; and my aunt often telling me to take my hands off my hips, and being mocked at school for the apparently non-masculine way that I stood and spoke.

As much as I tried not to let such comments bother me (they were just comments after all!), they really got under my skin, leaving me with a feeling that I just wasn't good enough; that there was something wrong with me; and that I needed to 'fix myself' if I wanted to be a real man.

And so, when, aged 24, I was on the phone to one of my best friends, and I said, 'I think I am broken', I really believed it. I felt as if I didn't have what it took to be a 'real man' – and so could never be someone that was loved, respected and looked up to.

Thankfully, I have grown a lot in self-confidence since then – largely due to spending so much time talking such issues through with my therapist and trusted friends. As a result, I now feel much more comfortable about who I am as a man.

However, during those younger years, I couldn't help but ask myself questions like ...

- What is wrong with me that I can't live up to what others expect of me as a man?
- How can I 'fix' myself and stop disappointing others?
- How come other men seem to fit in and do well? Yet I'm never good enough, or manly enough?
- What will it take for me to be respected and loved by others?
- Why am I not allowed to just 'be' who I am? And might there be ways that I can start to feel more at ease with myself?

As I mulled over questions like these in preparation to write this book, I remembered speaking to a man who had one of the most remarkable stories I had ever heard of going from feeling lost and broken in life, to being happy and confident in his full, authentic self.

ANOTHER PERSPECTIVE

Fifty-six-year-old Kenny Marmarella-D'Cruz was described in *Newsweek* magazine as the 'Man Whisperer', on account of him being 'a gentle voice in the ears of the many men who come to him for help'.

Kenny runs a group called MenSpeak for men of all backgrounds to come together and speak about the issues they face in their day-to-day lives, encouraging them to take ownership of their wellbeing by addressing traumas that they have historically been taught to avoid.

His own upbringing in Uganda was extremely traumatic. At first he had enjoyed what he described as a pretty idyllic childhood. But terror then arrived in the form of dictator Idi Amin, who wanted to expel Indo-Ugandans, like Kenny and his family, from the country.

At the age of seven, Kenny was smuggled out of the country, along with his mother and five-year-old brother, and sent to a resettlement camp in England, while his father stayed behind to fight the cause in Uganda. His father couldn't initially leave the country as he was on the Ugandan Secret Service death list for helping people with paperwork and stopping near-death beatings in the post office he ran.

On departure, Kenny's father said to him, 'You may never see me again. You are the man of the family now, so take care of your mother and brother.' A lot of pressure for a seven-year-old! A pressure that would weigh on him for many years to come, even well into adulthood – long after his father had managed to escape and join them in the UK.

So what did this notion of being 'the man of the family' really mean to Kenny at such a young age?

The men he was seeing on the news in Uganda were soldiers – fighting, raping and pillaging. And he knew from his mother and grandmother that many of the men in their own family had had a lot of problems that had left them unable to properly take care of their families; his mother, therefore, used to plea with Kenny not to be 'like those other men … and to look after [them]', in ways the other men were not able to.

As Kenny said, 'That made little to no space for me to be my *own* man', particularly on top of the symptoms of post-traumatic stress disorder that were starting to emerge within him, and which he kept to himself as 'a dirty little secret' because he felt so broken.

It took Kenny many years to learn to just *be*, without the heavy expectations that his upbringing had placed upon him.

He learned to accept that *he* had never been broken in the first place, rather that he had, sadly, just been in a 'broken' *situation* through no fault of his own.

It wasn't until Kenny was well into his thirties that he truly began to experience himself as the more multifaceted, self-loving man he now is. 'I had to stop surviving and start living.' He said, 'I learned to move from shame and blame, to naming what was going on for me, from my own experience and feelings.'

Therapy wasn't on the agenda at the time, as 'it was seen as something for the wealthy, so the initial talking was with myself. Then the men's groups came much later, as I wanted to meet my male friends at depth ...'

Rather than buying into any kind of 'real man agenda' of having to be everything to everybody, at the expense of not being real to himself, Kenny had decided somewhere along his journey to just *be* the best Kenny he could be.

And this is now what he encourages the men in his MenSpeak groups to do, too – to be the best version of *themselves* that they can be. 'It's about loving ourselves in both the darkness and lightness of our masculinity, no matter where we sit on the spectrums created for us,' he says. 'It's about opening up space for us to feel accepted and loved, respecting one another's perspectives and experiences, and generating a willingness to talk about these identities … It's [about] *being* together, rather than *doing* together.'

ON REFLECTION

Realizing There is Nothing Wrong with Us
It is interesting that despite the extremely different circumstances in the two stories just told – me in a comfortable home environment in England, and Kenny tragically displaced from his home in Uganda – Kenny and I ultimately ended up going on similar emotional journeys. We both went from feeling that we were inadequate and broken, unable to live up to our society's expectations of us as men, to realizing that there was nothing wrong with us in ourselves.

I was *not* too 'soft' or 'flimsy', and there was *no* right or wrong way for Kenny to look after his mum and brother. These were myths that we had been choosing to take on board from other people, which were harming our perceptions of ourselves. We needed to take a step back from these myths in order to find our own space to grow and thrive.

It was only once we were each able to find this safe space to open up and just *be* our authentic selves – rather than pushing so hard to *do* all sorts of things in an attempt to please others – that we could start to see the value of our own core natures.

Creating Space for Ourselves

Another incredible man that I talked to about going on a journey of self-discovery from feeling lonely and inadequate to feeling connected and abundantly loved is 51-year-old psychotherapist and author Owen O'Kane.

Owen shared his experience of growing up in Northern Ireland during the Troubles, when there was no shortage of what many considered to be 'real men' out fighting one another – taking action in the name of a cause.

He grew up in a Catholic family in Belfast with three 'blokey' brothers and a stoic father, in an environment where it was just presumed that guys would be tough, sporty men, with aspirations to have a wife and kids at some point down the line.

As Owen came to the realization that he was gay, he certainly didn't feel that he would be in any way accepted or nurtured for who he was in his immediate environment. He remembered the notion of wanting to 'fix' himself, or change himself for his own survival, always being at the forefront of his mind.

When he acknowledged in his twenties that he was going to have to come out as gay, he experienced what he called 'a real conflict' between wanting to fit in with, and be accepted by, the community around him, and wanting to just be able to be *himself*. He knew he would never be happy going down the heteronormative route just to keep everyone happy, but he wasn't sure what to do.

So, in his early twenties, he took the bold move of joining a Catholic monastery in Dublin, with the main motivation being to find out who he was for himself and his place in the wider world, away from his immediate circumstances. He found the experience of the monastery to be an immensely valuable one, coming to deeply value the art of mindfulness and meditation. After three years he felt steady enough in himself to go back to Belfast and come out to his parents. 'I came to the idea that I'd rather live truthfully and authentically than tell a lie and keep it from them,' he said.

By his mid-twenties he had become a palliative care nurse and when he was 39 he trained as a psychotherapist. From his working life, he realized just how many men struggle with their emotions, especially when coming to the end of their lives. He found that his own journey of discovery, where he had taken ownership of allowing himself to *just be*, was hugely instrumental in him being able to help others through their most difficult times.

Owen also used his experiences to write a bestselling book entitled *Ten To Zen*, which guides readers in how taking just ten minutes out of the day to allow yourself to *just be* can make such an enormous difference to your overall mental clarity and peace of mind.

'Culturally, we believe men should respond in a particular way and that there are certain emotions that are deemed more acceptable for men,' he says. 'But ultimately, we can't force people to be what *we* want them to be. We need people to naturally come to who they are. We need to allow them to just be.'

> ### Note to Self
> *How many things do I think I must try to fix,*
> *Until I realize that fixing things*
> *Isn't always what's needed?*
> *What's often needed is to just let them be.*

RETURN TO CONNECTION

Seeking Clarity: We Are Enough

Going back to My Point of Connection story I shared on page 75 about the effect on me of of being told to 'man up' and the like, I can now see that I went through many years of not believing I had much to offer the world because I viewed myself as a 'chipped mug' of sorts. As a result, I tried my hardest to be someone I wasn't – someone who was bold, super-decisive and ultra-dynamic.

Returning to the questions that I found myself posing in my own head after such experiences …

- *What is wrong with me that I can't live up to what others expect of me as a man?*
- *How can I 'fix' myself and stop disappointing others?*
- *How come other men seem to fit in and do well? Yet I'm never good enough, or manly enough?*
- *What will it take for me to be respected and loved by others?*
- *Why am I not allowed to just 'be' who I am? And might there be ways that I can start to feel more at ease with myself?*

… I now realize that:

- There was never *anything* 'wrong' with me. The problem was other people's fixed notions of masculinity being projected on to me, making me *feel* like there was something wrong with me for not fitting the mould. There simply are no right or wrong ways to be a man.
- My belief that there was a need to somehow change or 'fix' myself to be a 'real man' was a false one. I am and I always will be 'enough' at core. Don't get me wrong, there's always room for improvement in life – in order to grow as people – but this kind of empowering self-enhancement is best done

on our own terms, rather than to try to serve the desires of others.

- Not all other men are necessarily 'doing well' or feeling like they 'fit in'. Many could well be struggling with issues of self-identity and self-confidence, just as much as you; but some are simply better at wearing the masks that hide their authentic selves.

- Ironically, while we are chasing the love and respect of others by trying to fit the mould of what we feel they *want* us to be, we are unlikely ever to feel authentic, connected or happy in ourselves. If, however, we can start to let go of the expectations that others project on to us, and simply learn to 'be' what we are at our own core, our authenticity will lead to self-love. And this self-love is likely to lead to the love and respect of valued people around us.

- It is not so much that I wasn't allowed to *be* but more that *I* wasn't allowing myself to be. When we are stuck as human *doings* we think of being human as an action, rather than a state. Viewing things in this way is unlikely to ever allow us to feel fully happy, as we'll always be too busy moving on to the next thing that needs to be done. But if we can switch to loving ourselves as human *beings*, we will have taken a huge step towards living a life of more love, belonging and connection.

What Do We Love About Ourselves?

I once had a therapy session where my therapist asked me to tell her some things I liked, or loved, about myself. She sat waiting in her chair as I stared at her, trying to think of something to say. I could feel the tears bubbling up in my eyes. 'I can't,' I struggled to say. 'I can't think of anything about myself that I like.'

She leaned forward and said gently, 'It's time to try. What positive qualities do you think you have? Search for them over the next few weeks, and we'll continue when you're back.'

The aim of this exercise was, of course, for me to start recognizing which of my core qualities I would be most happy to embrace in order to defy the programming that we have been so used to hearing from potentially detrimental influences around us. As my therapist kindly explained, we will never rise higher in the world than the way we see ourselves, so it's important to start forming a positive view of ourselves as soon as possible.

It's up to us to keep remembering that, despite what some others may try to tell us ...
We are not broken.
No-one is perfect.
We are all learning.

So, take the pressure off yourself.

You are doing just fine, wherever you are on your journey.

LEARNING TO LOVE OUR AUTHENTIC SELVES

As we've discussed, recognizing our *own* positive qualities can feel challenging at first if we have spent years trying to hide our true selves under a mask of what we feel 'should' be as men. But starting to view ourselves through a kinder, more compassionate lens – whether we are gentle, sensitive and introspective, bold, boisterous and extroverted, or whatever else – is the only way that we'll ever feel more comfortable in our own skin, and achieve the authentic, meaningful life most of us are keen to have.

MY POINT OF CONNECTION

I was often teased at secondary school – for being smart, bookish, quiet, sensitive, or a host of other things along the same lines. Because I was a tall, Black boy (already 6 foot at 14), there seemed to be an expectation that I would be tough and intimidating. Instead, I was shy, kind and friendly, which seemed to confuse people. Some students took to calling me the BFG – the 'Big

Friendly Giant'. Others (I have since been told) took this a step further – to the 'Big Friendly Gay'.

Once, when I was 16, a guy at school picked a fight with me. I remember to this day, not only the feeling of confusion that he had done this in the first place, but my absolute dread at the feeling that I needed to retaliate to show him that I couldn't be pushed around.

In that same year, I was so annoyed when I overheard someone in the hallway taunt me about what I was wearing, that I saw red and punched him in the face before I even had a chance to think about it. The boy's older brother was in my year group, and I thought it was going to cause a huge fight, so I went to my head of year, and explained what happened, fully expecting to get in trouble. But I was just sent home with the message that 'There was no need for me to stay as it might escalate'.

By the time I got home, my dad was waiting (he had gotten a call from the school). He told me I was sensible for coming home and not to worry – that everyone sees red sometimes. He added, 'If you let people say these things about you, you have no choice but to believe them.' So, in the end I was very much left with the sense that 'boys will be boys' – and that it was almost expected that a young teenage guy like myself would fight back if their masculinity was in any way challenged.

It seemed to me that my authentic self – who didn't like confrontation or aggression, and who didn't see the point of

getting into fights – wasn't welcome in any of these scenarios.
Instead, I had to try to play the traditional tough guy role expected
of me in order to prove myself to everyone.

Thankfully, I learned as I got older and got to know myself
better that I didn't need to rise to such occasions in order to
prove anything. I learned that I could instead choose to just
brush comments off and walk away, in the knowledge that
violence of any kind, for any reason, doesn't sit with my core
values in life, and that I'd rather lead a life of self-acceptance,
love and compassion.

But at the time, I couldn't help but ask myself questions like ...

- *Why am I being forced into this 'tough guy' role that I don't fit?*
- *Why can't I just be myself and be accepted for that?*
- *What am I trying to prove to people by putting on a show of being boisterous and tough?*
- *Why am I feeling so frustrated and angry about it all?*
- *Are there ways that I could react to such situations in the future that would allow me to feel truer to myself?*

ANOTHER PERSPECTIVE

It wasn't until I was older that I realized I wasn't alone in having
these feelings of needing to try to be something other than
myself in order to feel like I had a valid place in life.

I met 29-year-old activist and writer Alexander Leon when he featured as a guest on my *Time To Talk* podcast. He spoke about the intensity of the internal dialogue that led him to 'come out' as a gay man to his family and live a life that was true to him. This was supported by a piece he wrote on his blog, called 'Out of the closet and into the fire – how I stopped performing and fought to become myself', about what *self*-acceptance looked like in the face of wanting to live an accepted life.

For Alex, growing up in a mixed-race household – of English and Sri Lankan heritage – in Australia, he had learned that his survival as a young, effeminate, brown boy, relied on play-acting.

Early on, he'd seen that little things he would do, like pick up a Barbie or try on girls' clothes, could raise eyebrows or even incite anger from the adults around him. As he got older, his teachers would chastise him for his femininity, and boys in his year would call him things like 'faggot' before he even knew what the term meant. 'So, in fear of their scrutiny,' he said, ' I made the world a theatre, and myself its stoic performer-in-residence. After all, if it was all pretend, I couldn't get hurt.'

Alex went into the performing arts as a teenager, but soon realized that 'the curtains never came down', to the point where he no longer felt he knew who or what his actual self was, as it had become so hidden behind the roles he played.

He describes this as 'sacrificing authenticity to minimize humiliation and prejudice'.

He said, 'I think … for a lot of us [gay people], before we realize that we are *actually* gay (if you take the term gay to mean same-sex attracted), we just realize that we are not quite adhering to the expectations of our gender.' As a child, he remembers thinking things like, 'I don't want to play with the boys, because they are rough', as he didn't identify with that. He would often want to sit with the girls who were chatting and playing with dolls – 'stuff I felt more comfortable doing'.

'If you think about that, it's quite off that you give children these "programmes" of how to be a boy and how to be a girl – like boys aren't allowed to cry, girls are allowed to cry. Girls are allowed to say this, and boys aren't allowed to say that. I think these have long-lasting effects when it comes to how you grow up – and how you show up and prove yourself to the world.'

Alex now views masculinity as a very fluid concept, accepting that you can be effeminate but still masculine. But it took him a long time to get to this point where he felt comfortable in what he had often previously thought was his *compromised* version of masculinity.

'The experience of the closet is essentially us pushing down parts of ourselves,' says Alex. 'For some people, it goes from like 0–100, because they very quickly find themselves and say, "Wait, I *am* this camp, limp-wristed person and that's who I am, and I'm gonna *own* that." And for others, it's more of a treacherous path or winding road. So many of us are still unlearning the idea that the way we are is undesirable and unlikeable …

'We're trying to undo a lifetime of behaviour that has become automatic to us, so we need to be more compassionate to ourselves.' And it's that compassion that Alex aims to share with other people too, both in his personal interactions and through his work as an activist, writer and all-round wholehearted human being.

ON REFLECTION

Getting Comfortable with Who We Are

Both Alex and I had to learn that it really is OK to *be*, and to *show*, the *real* us even if some people might not like all our qualities, or might not deem them as 'manly' enough – whether our gentleness, our sensitivity, our creativity, or anything else. In learning to no longer hide all these aspects of our true selves, we start to treat ourselves with the compassion we all deserve in life. And only once we are able to fully embrace and love ourselves in this way, will we be able to extend this love outwards and attract it from others, too.

Daring to be Our Compassionate Selves

Another man I met with an interesting journey to a life of compassion was 33-year-old Jimmy Westerheim, founder of The Human Aspect, a company that seeks to improve mental health conversations around the globe by giving people the courage to reach out and share their personal stories.

Jimmy grew up in Norway, where he was surrounded by typically 'manly' men. Like myself, he was tall and athletic, but was picked on at school 'for being perceived as more feminine than the others'.

He recalled arriving home one day, feeling angry and upset that he was being bullied, and wanting to beat up the perpetrator. But his stepfather said to him, 'What do you think is going to happen if you beat him up? It probably won't stop because it is going to confirm his world, and he will pick on you more to get a reaction. He might have his own problems … so are you going to do that to him?'

He gave Jimmy the advice to 'Stay true to who you are – a gentle human, kind and compassionate. After all, would you rather be *like* the bully, or be different?'. He made it clear that the choice was Jimmy's.

Ever since then, every time Jimmy has ever got really angry with another person, he has thought about this conversation with his stepfather and reminded himself that he is better than that, and that he has the choice to 'treat the situation with compassion, as well as give some compassion to myself'.

As time went on for Jimmy, more and more of his life experiences – from a cancer scare that his mum went through when he was still a teenager, to him later badly injuring his back – taught him that it was best to keep breaking down the outer layers of toughness in order to really connect with the fullness of life, in its low moments as well as its high ones. And as he did so (with the help of some good therapy), his innate compassion and gentleness became his guiding light, revealing a new man – or maybe an original man – who was ready to face anything with love, truth and compassion.

Now, he says, he views his masculinity as 'nurturing, being true to who you are *and* saying, "Yes, I'm a man and I experience *all* kinds of emotions". I dare to be myself fully.'

What is There *Not* to Love About Being Authentic?

When we dare to be ourselves fully, we can do anything. When the people we look up to – parents, relatives, friends and colleagues – allow us to be ourselves, the sky's the limit.

This is what I found in Ted Bunch, dad to four boys and co-founder of A CALL TO MEN – an organization created to help shape a world where all men and boys are loving and respectful, and all women and girls are valued and safe.

A CALL TO MEN does this by hosting workshops on things like anti-bullying, and the prevention of domestic and sexual violence.

In the name of challenging what they refer to as the collective socialization of men, A CALL TO MEN encourages workshop participants to imagine what they call a 'Man Box' full of the toxic and often limiting views of masculinity that tend to be passed from generation to generation of men (whether consciously or not) and reinforced by society – and to then imagine themselves *unpacking* this box, so as to relieve themselves of the heavy pressures and expectations that come with the limitations.

Ted explained to me that not only does he try to live outside of this 'Man Box' himself, but that he also urges his four sons to do the same. He encourages them to fully embrace their authentic selves, as they were *born* to be – free of any preconceived collective societal notions of how they 'should' be.

As an example of this in action, Ted shared with me that, when his youngest son, Jalen, came out at 15 (something that came as no surprise to Ted), he not only embraced the news fully but celebrated it with him.

He also told me a beautiful story about he and Jalen travelling on public transport to a Gay Pride event. Jalen was wearing a rainbow cape and socks, and had his stomach painted in glitter. As they sat on the train together, a man approached Ted and said, 'It's wonderful that you support your son,' to which, instead of replying with the automatic and polite 'Thank you' that might have been expected, Ted said, 'What is there not to support?'

The curtain was up. Everything was out in the open. They were momentarily two heroes sitting together – being courageous and compassionate for one another, and inspiring others in the process.

Seeing Compassion as an Asset

Another fascinating man I met who spoke powerfully about the importance of men being able to openly show their compassionate side was Major Sam McGrath. Major McGrath is a highly decorated former paratrooper, now in his forties, Managing Director of a FTSE-100 company, devoted father to four young daughters, and a pro-level ultra-marathon runner.

Sam grew up in the north of England, joined the British Army on leaving school at 16 and went on to become one of the youngest British soldiers since World War II to achieve the esteemed rank of 'major'. He toured Northern Ireland, Iraq and Afghanistan, and, by 28, was in charge of 250 men in the elite Parachute Regiment. No small feat!

When he decided to leave the Army in 2010 – to devote more time to his family – he found it interesting to see just how much he was able to draw from his experience in the military to offer compassionate support and leadership in a family environment, too.

People tend to think of a job in the military as classically 'tough' and 'manly' – full of decisiveness, danger and bravado – but he points out that it's also one that requires a great deal of teamwork and, in his role, compassion too. He had to consider the safety of *all* his men, as well as himself, and, sadly, sometimes had to break the devastating news of loss of life to the families of men he had both led and toured alongside.

The sense of compassion that he developed for others also gave him more compassion for *himself*, including a heightened awareness of his own needs – something that was encouraged by his much-trusted mentor at the time, too.

He also noticed that his time as a paratrooper had given him a strong sense of what is called 'servant leadership', which meant that it felt completely natural for him to devote the same level of 'service' to his wife and four daughters now that he was at home.

'It's important to me,' he said, 'that I am compassionate with both myself and my family, to make sure that we are all emotionally supported. It's the only way we can break this mould of toxic ideals that often come with … masculinity.'

It's so useful to have men like Sam to look to for inspiration if ever we need a reminder that qualities such as compassion and sensitivity really are assets in life, and are by no means anything to ever shy away from.

> ### Note to Self
> *It's difficult to spend time with a person you don't love.*
> *So, it's time to try loving the person I was born to be.*
> *I meet myself with compassion,*
> *I am living life to my calling.*

RETURN TO CONNECTION

Seeking Clarity: We Have Nothing to Prove

Going back to My Point of Connection story on page 87, where I shared my experiences of feeling like I had to put on a show of bravado in order to fit in at school, I can now see that some of my reactions weren't ideal at the time, as they led to me feeling deeply frustrated at myself. However, it took me to have such experiences as I was growing up in order to get to know my true self better in the first place. Only once I started to really know my own truths and understand the value of living according to them, could I start to properly appreciate myself, love myself and live a more authentic, connected, compassionate life.

Returning then to the questions that I found myself posing in my own head after those school experiences …

- *Why am I being forced into this 'tough guy' role that I don't fit?*
- *Why can't I just be myself and be accepted for that?*
- *What am I trying to prove to people by putting on a show of being boisterous and tough?*
- *Why am I allowing myself to feel so frustrated and angry about it all?*
- *Are there ways that I could react to such situations in the future that would allow me to feel truer to myself?*

… I now realize that:

- Unfortunately a lot of people have preconceived notions of what they think other people 'should' be like, based on things like physical appearance. In this instance, my school mates were projecting their own misguided beliefs about young Black guys from my area of London being 'tough guys' and didn't want to accept anything different to that norm.
- I had been *trying* to be myself by being kind and friendly, but when this ended up being mocked, it reinforced the feeling already within me that my *authentic* self wasn't something that was likeable as a man. At a certain point, I felt it was better to suppress my true self out of a fear of being further mocked or rejected.

- I was trying to prove that I could be as tough and resilient as the next man if required, as I felt at the time that this was what was needed for people to see me as a 'real man' and therefore to stop making fun of me and show me some respect. I now know, of course, that my behaviour didn't 'prove' anything as there was never anything to prove in the first place.

- It is difficult to *not* feel frustrated and angry in situations where you're being picked on, especially when your manhood is being challenged, as I felt mine was. You feel frustrated and angry, not only that *others* are unfairly putting you in this situation, but that you are letting it affect both how you behave and how you feel about yourself. There is great pain and disconnect involved in not being able to be authentically you.

- It's important to get to really feel secure in both your authentic self and how this person fits into your wider view of masculinity, so that the next time either of these things is challenged, you know where you stand and what your boundaries are. If you're tempted to react in a way that instinctively feels wrong, or like some kind of performance, it's OK to stop and ask yourself, 'Why am I doing this? What do I have to prove?'

The answer to this question should always be:
I have nothing to prove. To anyone.

I am 'enough' just as I am.
I can dare to be myself. Fully. And authentically.
I love myself. Fully. And authentically.
And I will treat both myself and others
With the compassion we all deserve.

REAL MEN – THE REALITY

It's Time to Drop the Myth That:
Real Men are fearless go-getters.

It's Time to Remember That:
Real Men dare to be, and to love, whatever form their true authentic self takes, be it a fearless go-getter, a shy, sensitive soul, or anything in between. Real Men know that compassion is a superpower as it allows us to treat both ourselves and others with the love we all deserve.

CHAPTER 3

FINDING STRENGTH IN VULNERABILITY
Time to Talk About Bravery

Male characters that we see on screen are so often guys who keep their emotions firmly hidden from sight in the name of bravery and 'manliness', whether James Bond, Tony Soprano or *Game of Thrones* characters like Ned Stark.

But what does being 'brave' really mean in this day and age? Isn't there an irony in the idea of men feeling too scared to show their vulnerability in a quest to appear 'brave' – as if they're not 'allowed' to show that they're real people, with real feelings? Wouldn't it show more strength if we could be brave enough to show *all* sides of ourselves, *including* our vulnerability, to those we trust and love?

In this chapter, we will look at:

• Why men find it so hard to be honest about their emotions; isn't it time we recognized how unhealthy it is to bottle everything up? How can we change things so that we feel more empowered to share where we're really at?

- Why is it still so often viewed as 'weak' for men to ask for help or cry? Isn't it time to reframe these things more positively, and allow more space for men to open up as their authentic selves?

Real Man Myth: 'Real Men Don't Cry'

BEING HONEST ABOUT HOW WE FEEL

When asked 'How are you doing?', I always used to respond with, 'I'm good.' I try not to now, as I've realized that 'good' is a state, not an emotion. Answering in this way meant that, without meaning to, I was putting on a mask based on what I felt I was *expected* to say, rather than expressing my true feelings, which I'd never really been encouraged to show. So, how can we start being more comfortable with being honest about where we're at emotionally?

MY POINT OF CONNECTION
In November 2019, a month before my 28th birthday, my grandmother passed away, aged 83.

Since September she had been in and out of the hospital, so we knew that she was ill. But, on the November night that she took her last breath, my heart still felt like it broke into a thousand little pieces.

She had lived a full, happy life. But that didn't stop me from feeling sad, of course. Sad that I would never get to hold her hand again, hear her laugh again, get another birthday card from her, have her scold me again for entering the pantry cupboard for snacks without her permission …

I spent a lot of time with my nana, and she was one of the few people who I felt really understood me, so losing her felt like losing a huge part of myself. I really struggled with the rawness of my grief after her passing, and broke down frequently. I still have a voice-note of myself talking out loud on a walk, as if speaking to her, and suddenly just bawling, as I crumple up against a wall – after which, I took myself to the cinema to try to take my mind off feeling so completely lost and heartbroken.

There was a strong sense of togetherness as a family as a result of the implicit understanding that we were living through a similar experience of loss. And I was lucky enough to have a lot of good friends around me who were kind and caring, too.

Yet, when anyone asked how I was doing, all I could muster up was a response something along the lines of 'OK' as I just didn't know what else to say. How could I possibly convey the level of devastation I was really feeling? How would people react if they saw me at my most vulnerable? I was frightened about what they would think of me breaking down like this.

As a result, I ended up feeling a deep sense of loneliness during this period, despite being surrounded by people who loved me.

Months later, the pain is much less raw. I really miss my nana, of course. But, thankfully, as time has passed, I've managed to find a way to at least talk about the paralysing sense of not being able to fully express my true feelings. And, ironically, as I've done this, it's allowed me to start talking more about the fact that I am, without doubt, still grieving. And I imagine I'll be grieving for quite a while.

However, I'm also starting to accept, with the help of other people, that that's OK. And that the vulnerability that comes with the grieving is OK, too – nothing to be either ashamed of or afraid of.

In the initial months after Nana's passing though, I couldn't help but ask myself questions like ...

- Is it normal for a man of my age to feel so very heartbroken after the loss of a loved one?
- Isn't death just an inevitable part of life that I should be able to 'deal with'? And move on from?
- Why am I so worried about what others will think of me if I open up to them about how very sad and lost I feel?

- *How come the other men in the family seem to be 'holding it together' better than me?*
- *Will I ever be able to pick myself up and move on from this? Will my heart ever mend from this?*

ANOTHER PERSPECTIVE

One man I spoke to about his experience of sadness and vulnerability was Daniele, a 47-year-old man of Italian descent. Daniele told me about the devastating loss of his younger brother, Andrea, from a brain tumour. He spoke, not just of the grief around losing him, which was, of course, immense, but of the struggles that came with knowing about Andrea's illness for years preceding his death. This included knowing that Andrea would no longer be around by the time of his wedding to long-term partner Tina.

After Andrea passed away at the age of 37 in 2011, Daniele felt like a broken mess and started dreading his wedding day the next year. And this made him feel he was hugely letting down Tina, as he wanted to be looking forward to it as the happiest day in their lives.

The day before the wedding, Tina gave Daniele a letter that changed how he viewed things. It read 'To My Future Husband. The time I felt closest to you was … 2011 – our *annus horribilis*. You have always shown strength, and I've always admired that about you. But this was the year I saw something I'd never seen in you before – and that was your vulnerable side. It doesn't come out very often, and all I wanted to do was look after you.'

On reading this, Daniele realized that showing his vulnerability to his partner in his darkest hours hadn't been letting her *down*, as he had feared. It had actually been bringing them closer together. Him having been brave enough to share his innermost feelings, cry with her and grieve with her had only served to deepen their connection and their love.

This was a huge turning point for him, allowing him to stop beating himself up about his grief. It didn't matter what age he was, what gender he was, or anything else. He was a human being with emotions, like all other human beings. And, as such, he was entitled to grieve and feel pain.

ON REFLECTION

Is There a Masculine Response to Grief?
According to the Centre for Human Potential, there are specific differences in current masculine and feminine approaches to grieving. Masculine grievers tend to keep to themselves when enduring a loss, not wanting to appear weak in the face of other people. They are seen to 'get on with' life, wanting to overcome the emotions quickly and 'fix' the situation. In comparison, feminine grievers want to feel their way through

the process, tell their story and seek a connection with both themselves and others about it.

To me, the key question here is, 'Why is this the case?' Do these behaviours stem from instinctive ways of being that are best for all concerned? Or is it more about learned behaviours passed down from generation to generation based on long-outdated myths about what it means to be a 'real man'? Personally, I think these are learned behaviours, and they and the resulting subconscious patterns are key when looking at men's relationship to emotional vulnerability.

The Value of Vulnerability

The more I have thought about my own and Daniele's experiences of bereavement, the more I see how vital it is that, instead of conforming to these outdated myths of stoic manliness, we start to *confront* our *fears* around showing emotions. We need to recognize the immense *value* in embracing our emotions and learning to be honest about them.

When we share our vulnerability with others in this way, it can help us to …

- feel less heavy – no longer having to bottle all our emotions up and carry them around without letting them rattle;

- feel more authentic – so that we're not wasting a lot of energy trying to hide our emotions all the time;
- stop feeling so lonely – with more of a sense of trust and belonging;
- potentially experience more of a sense of connection with our loved ones – as we get to know each other on a deeper level.

Why *Wait* to Open Up?

It's interesting to notice that both examples of learning about the power of emotional vulnerability explored so far are situations that involve the loss of a loved one.

This makes me think of my 13-year-old self nervously telling my maternal grandfather, 'I love you' in the last few days of his life, and him returning with 'I love you too, grandson.' This was the first time I had heard those words from him.

It also makes me think of my uncle Danny, who died from sepsis at 60, and was only able to admit how 'fucked up' he really felt at the point he was punctured with tubes and hooked up to a life-support machine. And of my cousin Richard, who threw a big 59th birthday barbecue for the family just months before he died of stomach cancer, but who chose not to share the sad news of his illness with any of us other than his wife and children.

Why is it that such good, loving men felt they had to maintain a façade of non-emotional 'bravery' and 'strength' almost to the very end? Surely it's not healthy that it should take something as extreme as a serious illness or death before we feel comfortable enough to talk honestly with our loved ones about how we're feeling! When did so much guilt and shame get attached to just telling our own truth? And why should we continue to let this be the pattern as we move forward in life?

Talk Before it's Too Late

Another person who realized the importance of learning to share our emotions sooner was mental health campaigner Ben West, who talked to me in 2019 about having lost his younger brother Sam to suicide just the year before.

Ben explained that it was the devastating impact his brother's death had on him that led him to do what he now does for a living. He first started the campaign PROJECT #WalkToTalk (now part of PROJECT:TALK) after Sam died in early 2018. The walks were designed to get people talking openly while walking, therefore promoting the idea that it is both OK to not be OK, and OK to *talk* about this, rather than waiting until things become desperate.

On seeing how much this project helped so many, he then went on to start #SaveOurStudents, a campaign that calls for the government to put in place mandatory mental health first-aid training for all UK teachers. He started this campaign after realizing just how many teachers felt unequipped with the tools to deal with the emotional problems faced by a lot of their students. The petition connected to this has more than 300,000 signatures as I write this.

Through both these successful campaigns, Ben has massively helped to raise awareness around mental health issues, encouraging young men, in particular, to take on board just how important it is to start talking, sharing – and therefore lightening their own burden – *before* things get to crisis point, rather than waiting until it's too late.

Emotional Fitness

Nick Bennett, a friend of mine, ended up going on a similar emotional journey in the wake of a close friend taking his own life.

'When he died, I was deeply upset. The night I found out, I went into my garden with a bottle of spirits, drank the whole bottle and then just cried and shouted at the mirror all night long … Then there was a period of denial and large waves of guilt … trying to figure out what more I could have done …'

But after a while, with the help of his wife Carien, Nick realized that he wouldn't have had the mental and emotional toolkit to help his friend, as he didn't really know how to communicate and understand emotions properly. Carien pointed out to Nick that he was 'a closed book', and that 'Strength isn't what you think it is. It's not about being closed up.'

He now muses, 'Growing up, we have physical education … but there is no mental education. Where was *that* class? … Teaching and practising skills like confidence and bravery through talking about your feelings – not keeping it to yourself?'

It was noticing this mental education gap in lifelong learning (both in educational institutions and in workplaces) that led to Nick to found and build the data-driven mental fitness platform Fika. The aim of Fika is to help young men and women develop the mental literacy to be able to both get in touch with and express their feelings confidently as they move through life, rather than only really noticing them once they're at an extreme.

> ### Note to Self
> *One thing I knew for sure: I feel things.*
> *One thing I didn't know: That I am allowed*
> *to be honest and show it.*

A RETURN TO CONNECTION

Seeking Clarity: We Don't Need Emotional Armour
Going back to My Point of Connection story on page 104 – about how heartbroken I was after the death of my nana –

I can now see that although I really struggled with the loss, I was doing the best I could at the time.

Although I didn't have the tools to reach out to others and *verbally* express the depth of my grief, I was at least able to take off my emotional armour when alone and express my grief through crying. I realize now that when I allowed this armour to come off, I felt lighter, I felt more authentic, I felt more comfortable with my own discomfort, and I felt freer.

Thinking about the kind of questions I was asking myself at the time of Nana's death then ...

- *Is it normal for a man of my age to feel so very heartbroken after the loss of a loved one?*
- *Isn't death just an inevitable part of life that I should be able to bravely 'deal with'? And move on from?*
- *Why am I so worried about what others will think of me if I open up to them about how very sad and lost I feel?*
- *How come the other men in the family seem to be 'holding it together' better than me?*
- *Will I ever be able to pick myself up and move on from this? Will my heart ever mend?*

... I can now see that:

- There was nothing unusual, weak or unmanly about me feeling such heartbreak. We *all* fear a loss in our lives, especially of the people we love most. It's natural to feel vulnerable and go through strong emotions at such times.
- Death is a natural part of the cycle of life, and we must be brave in acknowledging this as a reality. But, there is no right or wrong way for us *all* to deal with either this or any other emotional upsets in life. Instead, it's important for each of us to simply be honest with where we're at and what we need.
- Men have been conditioned through generations to see the sharing of emotion as weak and 'girlie'. As such, it's not uncommon for us to have unconscious worries that we might be rejected if we show our more vulnerable side. The key is to feel the fear and do it anyway!
- Even those seemingly 'holding it together' on the outside may or may not feel 'together' on the inside. We all deal with things differently – and that's OK.
- Grief isn't something we should feel like we have to 'move on from' or 'get over'; it's something to move *through* and learn from, like any deeply emotional experience. The good news is that the pain gradually lessens, and all the more so if you can just accept and admit your vulnerability, instead of trying to suppress it.

Now, I allow myself to fully feel. I allow myself to say how I am honestly feeling.

I seek people to connect with. I reach out.

I dig deep and allow myself to hear what is happening inside of me.

And to me, that is bravery.

It's time for us men to really take on board that being open about our emotions can be a great strength, and not the weakness we have been subconsciously conditioned to think of it as.

Maybe it would help to think of it as taking off a long-worn suit of emotional armour, which, as much as it might *appear* to protect us and make us look strong, can ultimately leave us feeling weighed down, unseen and disconnected from those around us. Part of removing this armour is addressing outdated macho perceptions that still surround things like men crying and asking for help – things that many men struggle with. So, let's turn to these topics next and explore how we can continue to break down the 'real man myths' surrounding them.

THE VALUE OF ASKING FOR HELP

There's a stereotype that when men get lost, they don't like to ask for directions; they'd rather just try to work it out for themselves, however fruitless that may prove. Unfortunately, this stereotype can carry over into the realm of emotions, too – many men, myself included, find it hard to ask for help when they're struggling. We believe that having to ask for help makes us weak or needy – which is the same worry I've experienced when I've cried in public.

But doesn't it seem mad – and deeply unhealthy – that in this day and age we should feel any sense of shame around simply expressing our emotions and needs? Why is it that, despite knowing, *rationally*, that it's healthy to be able to express ourselves, we are still subconsciously affected by the traditional 'manly' expectation to hold things together – and therefore *not* cry or ask for help?

MY POINT OF CONNECTION

I have a strong memory from when I was ten of really struggling with long division at school. I remember my frustration rising as my friends all seemed to get it and I just couldn't. But I felt too embarrassed – or maybe I just didn't know how – to ask for help. Before I knew it, my frustration took the form of tears and I was crying in front of the class.

My teacher pulled me aside and demanded I tell her why I was crying. But when I explained, as best as a ten-year-old could between splutters, instead of helping me and reassuring me, she got angry. She said I shouldn't be crying just because I couldn't do something – I should just 'get on with it'.

I also have a strong memory of waking up crying violently one night when I was 23, feeling a mixture of sadness, anger and suffocation all jumbled together in the pit of my stomach as I felt so lost in life at the time. I held myself tightly as I felt that there was no-one else in the world who could hold me in the way I needed, no-one I could ask for help, and no-one who could really understand what I was going through.

When I consider these events now, I can't help but ask myself …

- *Why did my teacher – someone in a supposedly caring profession – feel it was OK to dismiss a crying ten-year-old boy?*
- *How did my teacher's reaction make me feel at the time?*
- *Did the experience affect me beyond that day?*
- *Why did (and do) I find it so hard to ask others for help? Why do I presume others won't understand me?*
- *Have I managed between school and now to develop any kind of healthier relationship with expressing my feelings and showing my vulnerability to those I love?*

ANOTHER PERSPECTIVE

When I talked to 29-year-old Tom from Brighton about whether he had ever had times when he struggled with the idea of showing his vulnerability, he shared with me his recent experience of being in an emotionally, and at stages physically, abusive relationship.

Tom had got together with a woman he met at work, and all had seemed well at first. But she gradually became more controlling and manipulative – commenting negatively about the way he looked, mocking his music, putting down his friends while trying to get him not to see them, and keeping him alienated from his family.

As things progressed, Tom's self-esteem plummeted and he felt more and more trapped, lonely, helpless and stuck. 'It made me feel very weak. Like I was just inept at being a man. Or a human.'

He can now see that he was just an unfortunate person who was being taken advantage of and needed help. But, at the time, his sense of worthlessness and shame meant he didn't feel he could tell anyone about his situation – he was scared of being judged and further rejected. 'I just didn't have the confidence to talk to my friends or family about it. And I didn't have that kind of closeness with my parents. Even my best friend of all time didn't know … Because I'm quite tall, I think I always kind of felt embarrassed that I was being hit, controlled and attacked by someone who was much smaller.'

It took a final violent outburst for him to take action. 'She couldn't stop slapping me. I was just trying to ascertain what I was doing that was making her so mad and I ended up calling my mum saying, "Mum, she's hitting me. That's the sound you can hear." She was yelling down the phone at my mum. And it was then that I was just like, I've got to go, you know, I've got to go. So, I left and there's been no real contact ever since.'

Tom felt pretty bad for quite a while after this relationship, and had trouble sleeping. But, after some initial resistance, he sought help in the form of CBT (cognitive behavioural therapy) where he was encouraged to talk about his feelings and express himself in a way he had never been able to before.

He credits having this space in which he could properly open up for the first time with getting him to where he is today. He is in a much better emotional space; in a healthy, stable relationship; and has developed an app called ROY that provides an online platform where people can share their problems and be offered support when they don't feel able to get the help they need offline.

ON REFLECTION

Overcoming the Fear of Rejection

There are few things worse than asking for help or being visibly upset and someone telling you to 'get over it' or 'get on with it', as my teacher did to me when I was ten. The last thing you need is for people of importance in your life – friends, family, your partner, a teacher, or whoever – to make you feel small when you're at your most vulnerable.

The more I think about this, the more I realize that the key to us being able to express ourselves more freely – whether crying, asking for help or whatever else – is for us all to create a space of emotional safety for one another, from childhood onwards. Because, if we don't feel safe, we'll always be fearful – afraid of not fitting in, afraid of not looking strong and, ultimately, afraid of rejection. And no-one wants to live in fear.

It's important to remember that we *all* cry and need help as babies and young children, so why are different expectations put upon us as we become adults?

Creating a Safe Emotional Space
Thankfully, there are men out there who are already creating safer spaces for boys to be more emotionally honest. One of these is Jason Wilson, youth leader and CEO of Yunion, a social outreach, non-profit organization that serves youths and families, and author of bestseller *Cry Like A Man*.

In 2016, a video of him went viral that showed him being emotionally supportive of a boy who was crying when struggling with the board-breaking task in his martial arts class. The lesson was that breaking through the board would represent breaking through the many obstacles and difficulties in life.

When the boy broke into tears, Jason said, 'It's OK to cry. We cry as men, son. But *why* are you crying? … You know in life, there's going to be things [that are] harder for you to do than other things? And … you're going to have to do [them] as a man regardless? So, I don't mind you crying, I cry a lot too. I don't know whether you are fearing that you might not make it … We all face that from time to time. As soon as we hit resistance, we want to stop because it's hurting … but we have to fight through … because it's going to be painful. Being a Black man in this country, you're going to … need mental fortitude, more so than physical strength.'

The boy felt heard, valued and safe. Jason ended with, 'It's good to cry so you can work through the difficult emotion. Then when it arises again, you know what you need to do to overcome it.' When the boy then tried again to break the board, he completed the task. Shame and fear of failure had been squashed, and safety had been maintained in that dojo.

We need more leaders like Jason who are willing to empower those around them with compassion and sensitivity, recognizing the great strength that we can find in facing up to our vulnerabilities.

Baring it All

My friend Ben Bidwell is a life coach who goes by the moniker The Naked Professor – 'naked' being a metaphor for how he encourages the people (mainly men) that he works with to 'bare it all' by being more open, honest and vulnerable about their inner life.

A strapping man, one of three brothers and a seasoned rugby player in his youth, Ben was very much brought up to be a 'man's man' in a world that didn't see the value in vulnerability. However, after going through a period in his twenties where he lived what he now views as a fairly toxic lifestyle, during which he bottled up his emotions and only connected with mates on a banter level, he realized that things needed to change if he was to ever feel more connected with people, and find his deeper sense of purpose in life.

On speaking to me about his journey to a more emotionally vulnerable life, Ben told me about a time when, at the age of 37, a particular song came on at an event he was attending, triggering a memory that made him cry. He remembers feeling grateful for and *empowered* by the beautiful emotions that the song evoked, and for being in a space where he felt safe enough to really connect with these emotions and express himself freely, rather than unhealthily pushing his feelings down and hiding them. It was a fantastic reminder to him of how far he had come.

He and his friend Richie Bostock, also known as The Breath Guy, have since hosted an event called *Answering The Call: Supporting the Minds of Men*. This event sought to bring men together, challenge traditional notions of masculinity and inspire more vulnerable living. Incorporating breathwork, mindfulness and a range of other activities, attendees were encouraged to speak about their emotions, embrace their tears and eradicate the shame around these things. As Ben says, 'It's a beautiful thing, emotion.'

Knowing We're Not a Burden

I noticed that a workshop I recently hosted on writing for emotional health was attended mostly by women, and just one man. The women in the group engaged in easy, flowing conversation when talking about what emotional safety was for them, while the man stayed silent. It was only when I asked for feedback at the *end* of the session, that he spoke up, through tears, saying, 'I'm so sorry I am so emotional. I wish I could be better and present myself better. I don't want to be a burden on anyone.'

This made me realize that I, too, have often felt like a burden on others in situations in which I felt upset and vulnerable.

Sometimes all we need is to be given the space – or to give *ourselves* the space – to talk and be heard – and to know that we're *not* a burden. We are *all* worthy of love, safety and care from others.

> ### Note to Self
> *I am not a burden for sharing when I am struggling,*
> *I am not less of a man for crying,*
> *I can ask for help when I need it.*
> *And I will feel lighter, freer and more connected for doing so.*

A RETURN TO CONNECTION

Seeking Clarity: We All Need Help at Times

Going back to My Point of Connection story on page 117 where I described times that I broke down in tears as a result of not knowing how to ask for the help I needed, I wish I could go back and tell my younger self that everything's OK, and there's no need to feel embarrassed about being frustrated and upset.

When I look at the questions that the events brought up in my mind …

- *Why did my teacher – someone in a supposedly caring profession – feel it was OK to dismiss a crying ten-year-old boy?*
- *How did this reaction to me crying in school make me feel at the time?*
- *Did the experience affect me beyond that day?*
- *Why did (and do) I find it so hard to ask others for help, choosing to presume they won't understand me?*
- *Have I managed between then and now to develop any kind of healthier relationship with expressing my feelings and showing my vulnerability to those I love?*

… I now realize that:

- The teacher who belittled me for crying when struggling in school was probably stuck within the framework of outdated 'real man myths' that we're challenging in this book, which makes it all the more important that we continue to challenge such myths.
- At the time, my teacher's reaction to my tears made me feel useless and deeply ashamed.
- The older I get, the more I believe that little events like this, when repeated in different settings throughout our

formative years, can have a really damaging longer-term effect on how we operate in personal relationships. This incident planted seeds of fear and lack of self-worth that I'm still trying to shake to this day, making it harder for me to open up to others.

- Asking others for help will always feel hard for people who have been raised to be independent, and for men who feel that they should be islands unto themselves. But it's important to remember that we humans are, in fact, interdependent creatures at the core, so we *all* need support from one another at times.

- I have worked hard throughout my twenties at embracing my more vulnerable side. As a result, I definitely feel more willing than before to ask for help when I need it, and I also feel less uncomfortable when I cry. However, I still have a long way to go before I can fully say that I feel *brave* in my vulnerability, so here's to keeping that torch lit moving forward.

If I *could* go back and speak to my younger self, I'd tell him that it's OK to *feel*.

There's nothing to be embarrassed, ashamed or afraid of.

In fact, it's *good* to feel.
It shows that you're alive and emotionally engaged with the world around you.

And it's good – and even *brave* – to be *honest* about those feelings by sharing your vulnerability, through crying or asking for help. Only then will we be able to move forward with less fear and more love in our hearts.

REAL MEN – THE REALITY

It's Time to Drop the Myth That:
Real Men don't cry.

It's Time to Remember That:
Real Men are strong enough to acknowledge their own feelings and talk or even cry about them when needed. Showing vulnerability in this way, and being willing to ask for help from the people we trust is the bravest thing we can do and allows for a deeper sense of love, belonging and connection in life.

CHAPTER 4

THERE'S NO BODY LIKE YOUR BODY
Time to Talk About Health and Body Image

Just like with emotional and mental health, there seems to be an inherent shame – masked as unwillingness and avoidance – when it comes to men talking about their physical health. While this book addresses men's lack of ease in terms of talking about their *emotional* and *mental* health, I'd also like to address matters of *physical* health and body image.

Why is it that men so often dismiss physical health issues, choosing not to prioritize things like nutrition, exercise and trips to the doctor, yet at the same time we see increasing numbers of body image and body confidence issues emerging among the male population?

In this chapter, we will look at:

- The importance of learning to listen to our bodies more – exploring how we can pay better attention to what they need and speak up about any health issues that arise. Wouldn't it feel good to be more actively engaged in our own health and longevity?

- The rising pressures around male body image – exploring how the increasing pressure for men to tend to their appearance is creating an unhealthy focus on *looking* good rather than *feeling* good. How can we build our body confidence based on our own standards rather than those of others?

Real Man Myth: 'Real Men Have No Worries About Their Bodies'

LISTENING TO OUR BODIES

Our bodies are truly incredible things, yet we so often take them for granted. Men, in particular, it seems, tend to treat their bodies as trusty machines that will never give up on them, forgetting that, in order to keep functioning, they will, of course, need regular care and maintenance, like any other 'machine'!

Why is it that we don't treat them with the awe and respect that they surely deserve by paying them a little more attention and listening to the signs when something needs to be addressed? It's time to open up more about our health – and embrace the part we can play in its maintenance and enhancement – so that we can have increased peace of both mind and body as we move forward in life.

MY POINT OF CONNECTION

These days I have a keen awareness of my body and its needs, and I try to take care of it in the best way I can. But this wasn't always the case.

As mentioned in the Introduction, when I was working at a busy national newspaper, aged 23, I was completely overdoing things and not paying proper attention to my body at all, or giving it the respect I now realize it deserves.

Early mornings. Late nights. Junk food lunches. Sugary snack after sugary snack to keep me going through the often long and arduous days. I was running on empty and ignoring the feelings of stress, weakness and exhaustion that were becoming an increasing part of my daily reality.

The insomnia, the inability to concentrate and the emerging body aches all kept getting worse. Then, one night in 2016, I completely broke down in my room. Everything felt like it was caving in around me. After a few days in bed, crying, I didn't know what else to do but to get back to work and carry on. I felt I couldn't speak to anybody about it, as I would be perceived as someone who couldn't do my job, or who was too fragile and should 'man up'.

A month or so later, the same thing happened again, and affected the way I recorded my podcast. I wasn't feeling good about myself at all.

But it wasn't until my third breakdown, which happened at work, that I knew I had to do something different if I wanted to break the cycle.

I now know that I was having a full-blown panic attack when I called my friend, in tears, to help calm me down that day. Thankfully, he encouraged me to go to the doctor, and various blood tests were done.

The results revealed I had a minor form of rheumatoid arthritis, which came as quite a shock given I was only 23! The doctor recommended I see a rheumatologist. However, as I gradually realized that the symptoms only ever flared up when I was particularly stressed, I learned that I could manage things pretty well simply by taking more care of myself – better diet, enough exercise, enough rest, lots of nice walks, calmer environments, etc. – all of which made me feel good!

This was a real wake-up call for me. I needed to listen to my body – it had been giving me plenty of signs over the years – and make some much-needed changes. It was a massive learning experience for me to see just how drastic an impact my emotional state had on my physical state!

Still, to this day, when I'm under particular stress and ignoring subtle signs from my body (whether headaches or leg *cramps), symptoms of rheumatoid arthritis can emerge, making it hard for me to get out of bed in the mornings.*

Thankfully, however, I now know certain steps I can take to start looking after myself when life gets out of balance: slowing down a little, observing what's going on in my life, spending more time in nature, mindful breathwork and meditation, as well as going to the doctor for advice when needed, of course!

However, at 23, I had to ask myself the basic questions:

- *Why did I ignore the signs that my body was giving me that it was under too much stress?*
- *Surely, as a man in my twenties, I should be stronger than this and able to deal with anything?*
- *Why don't my friends and colleagues with similar lifestyles seem to be struggling with their health in the same way as me?*
- *Why did I wait for so long before seeking help?*
- *How can I take better care of my health, both physical and emotional, moving forward?*

ANOTHER PERSPECTIVE

One aspect of my health that I neglected for a long time was nutrition – which I now know is a vital piece of the health puzzle. I talked to nutritional therapist and author Ian Marber, who speaks and writes a lot about men's attitudes to food in particular.

In his book *Man Food*, a nutritional guide for men over 40, he says, 'I do think there's a certain machismo left over when it comes to men's health and wellbeing – especially with older men. There's that whole, "Oh that? It is all fuss and nonsense, I don't need to worry myself with that."'

Ian explained to me how, when his father read his book, he quipped that it felt like 'an instruction manual for something he doesn't actually *own*'. Ian finds this kind of dissociation from what the body needs troubling – reflective of a lack of either ability or willingness among many men to tune into, and listen to, their own bodies as a means of self-preservation and self-care.

'Is self-care effeminate?', he asked as our chat continued. 'I don't think so at all …', he said, '… and men need to stop thinking it is, as we all benefit from it.'

Ian reminded me that prostate cancer is the third biggest cancer in the UK (ahead of breast cancer), and one in eight men will be diagnosed with it. He is of the opinion that this is at least 'partly because men are less concerned – we don't go to the doctor as often, we are less likely to have preventative tests.

'If I had one piece of advice [as a nutritionist], I'd say don't take your health for granted. The same way we monitor our finances, understanding pensions, etc., we [also] need to invest in our health.'

ON REFLECTION

Be Grateful for Your Body; it's the Only One You've Got

Many men treat what they feel are minor ailments as annoyances that they hope will go away if they ignore them for long enough. Young men, in particular, tend not to listen to the symptoms until something goes *really* wrong, physically or emotionally.

It would be amazing if we could shift this perception so these same men were more appreciative of what their bodies allow them to do, and be, each day. Things like eating well, getting enough exercise, asking for help and going to the doctors when health issues come up could then simply be viewed as a means of showing gratitude and respect for these bodies (without which, let's face it, we'd all be pretty lost!).

Conversations with Doctors

When I interviewed Dr Earim Chaudry, GP and medical director of men's wellness brand, Manual, for my podcast, I asked him to share some of the insights he had gotten into men's attitudes to health as a result of his direct contact with patients at his surgery.

He talked about how, once men finally swallow their pride and get to the surgery, there are often then challenges due to them being 'very evasive' about the main issues in hand.

So, for example, if a man is struggling with mental health issues, he is unlikely to come and say, 'I've got a mental health problem.' Instead, he might mention a whole list of other, non-specific symptoms (stress at work, insomnia, drinking more than usual …). Then, near the end, as they're going towards the door, they'll say, 'Oh! And Doctor …'

Dr Chaudry talked about the importance of *recognizing* just how difficult it can feel for men to open up about health issues, even though, to doctors, the issues they're bringing up are likely to be very common.

He said, 'If everybody could just *speak* about things, safe in the knowledge that there would be compassionate listening, without judgement, then maybe men wouldn't bottle up and explode the way so many of them do, and maybe there would be less men reaching crisis point as a result.'

In 2008, the US Agency for Healthcare Research and Quality launched a 'Real Men Wear Gowns' campaign, with the aim of convincing men to don hospital gowns and get screened for various cancers and other chronic diseases. Among other recommendations, the campaign offered tips on how to talk to doctors. Men's health researcher Wizdom Powell Hammond PhD MPH said, 'We have to frame health-care seeking as an act of self-reliance. The message should be that taking charge of your health is what it means to be a real man. You have decision-making power about your health.' This is a clear and powerful message and one that deserves to be listened to.

Alternative Approaches

If we acknowledge just how much our physical health can impact our emotional health, and vice versa, it's worth being open to exploring approaches to health and self-care that haven't traditionally been part of the Western medical approach – what many call 'alternative health' practices.

One example of this can be seen in the health journey of the dad of a friend of mine, Richie Bostock.

Richie's dad was diagnosed with the autoimmune disease multiple sclerosis (MS), for which there is no cure as yet. 'It's a thing you have to learn to deal with,' explained Richie, 'so I was always on the lookout for alternative therapies and lifestyle changes that might be able to help.'

During this search, Richie came across the work of Dutch extreme athlete Wim Hof, also known as The Iceman, who has become known for his unconventional approaches to enhancing health and overcoming disease.

Richie decided to sign up for one of Wim's retreats to get exposure to the Wim Hof Method for himself – a method that includes chiefly breathwork and exposure to extreme cold, with a view to regaining control over both body and mind (mind over matter!).

'The retreat started with a hike in our shorts in the area surrounding the hotel at -3ºC. And the week that ensued was then full of Wim Hof's crazy but super invigorating techniques, including sitting in ice-cold lakes and hiking barefoot in the snow. At the end of the week we then all climbed Mount Sněžka, on the Polish/Czech border – technically, the tallest mountain in Czech Republic, but we climbed it from the Polish side.'

'There were 25 people,' Richie told me. 'Men, women, young, old, fit, not fit. And everyone made it to the top of that mountain. As well as got through the entire week. No-one even got as much as a sniffle!'

'It was really impactful. I mean, the cold stuff … just blows your mind, but what was really impactful for me was the breathwork. I just remember thinking, how crazy is it that not everyone knows that people can feel this way just by doing a little bit of breathing. So that was what stuck with me.'

When Richie returned home, he showed his dad lots of photos from the trip and told him all about it, including the amazing rejuvenating and life-affirming impact he had seen all the 'crazy' techniques having on the various attendees.

His dad saw something special in the idea of opening up to such alternative approaches and decided to try the home version of the method for himself – having cold showers every day, doing regular breathing exercises and changing his diet in a big way (important for any autoimmune disease).

Incredibly, not long after he started regularly practising the techniques, there was no further progression of the MS – it just seemed to stop it in its tracks! 'So that was pretty crazy for my family,' Richie said.

Richie's dad is coping well with his condition now. So inspired was Richie that he went on to study and train in breathwork himself. He is now a successful teacher who goes by the moniker The Breath Guy, and has written his first book, *Exhale*.

Take a Breath

According to Richie, breathwork is simply about becoming aware of our breathing and working out how to use it or to change it to create some physical, mental or emotional benefit for ourselves. As such, it can be an immensely useful self-care and health enhancement tool.

He says people often ask him, 'Why would I need to just work on my breathing?', as they view it as something that just happens, which means they tend to take it for granted. 'But what people don't realize is that the way we breathe affects every single system and function in the body, whether that be the nervous system, immune system, endocrine system, digestive system. …'

Learning how to breathe correctly (i.e. deeply), and how to use the breath to tune into the body, become more aware of it and address any internal pain and trauma can therefore help us to remember what really matters when it comes to our health. Sometimes, it's just as simple as taking a breath, and remembering that our health is the most important thing we have.

> ### Note to Self
> *My health is the most important thing I have.*
> *It's time I treated it like the friend it is,*
> *The loyal one that never leaves,*
> *The one that is always there and*
> *should be handled with care.*

A RETURN TO CONNECTION

Seeking Clarity: Our Health Is Our Wealth

Going back to My Point of Connection on page 131 – where I thought about a time in my life where I really neglected my health and paid the consequences, I can now see that if I hadn't gone through that, I wouldn't have learned the importance of taking better care of my health and being more willing to seek help when needed. And I wouldn't feel so passionate about encouraging *other* men to do the same …

Thinking back to the kind of questions I was asking myself at the time of my panic attack at work ...

> - *Why did I ignore the signs that my body was giving me that it was under too much stress?*
> - *Surely, as a man in my twenties, I should be stronger than this and able to deal with anything?*
> - *Why don't my friends and colleagues with similar lifestyles seem to be struggling with their health in the same way as me?*
> - *Why did I wait for so long before seeking help?*
> - *How can I take better care of my health, both physical and emotional, moving forward?*

... I now realize that:

- I ignored the signs that my body had been giving me to slow down as I didn't want to make an unnecessary fuss. I just kept telling myself it was 'probably nothing'. But ignoring our bodies when they're under stress isn't smart, as, if we don't acknowledge our symptoms, they are likely to just keep getting worse until we're *forced* to listen at crisis point.
- Every human body has its own strengths and weaknesses – a combination of what we were born with and

the learned habits that have become ingrained as we've grown up. Just because someone is in their twenties doesn't necessarily mean that they 'should' be stronger or fitter than an older person. Anyway, strength is more than just a physical thing; strength in a health context also means being brave enough to acknowledge when issues arise and being sure that we take the best next steps to restore optimal wellness.

- My guy friends might *seem* like they're all fine figures of health on the *outside*. But how would I know how they *really* are beneath the surface, given we so rarely talk about such 'personal' matters? Wouldn't it be refreshing to drop any sense of embarrassment and worry around talking about something as vital as our health? Instead, we should lean on one another for support around such issues, as women often do.

- If I'm honest with myself, my main underlying reason for waiting so long before going to the doctor was fear. Fear of appearing weak. Fear of not looking like a 'real man'. And fear of what I might find out and then have to confront. But going to see the doctor was a courageous step in the right direction as it allowed me to know where I stood, and I could then take positive action from there.

- I can take better care of my health moving forward by simply becoming more aware of what's going on not only in my body and in my mind, but also by trying to notice how each of these entities is impacting on the other. Once I'm more tuned into my health on this holistic level, I can start to trust what feels right and what doesn't, and therefore not force my body to do things that it may not have the energy or capacity to do at that time.

When I think back to how I allowed myself to ignore my stress levels while working in the newsroom, I realize how silly it was. Not only did it cause me undue pain, both physical and emotional, but it could have jeopardized my future had I let it continue. What use would my hands be to me as a writer if they were seized up due to the rheumatoid arthritis that was developing?

We need to take the time for ourselves and truly listen to our bodies if we are going to get more connected to who we are.

In summary then, our precious human body is vitally important to our everyday existence.
So, let's try not to take it for granted.
Let's instead appreciate it
And be grateful for it.

Let's try to eat well, rest well,
Drink plenty of water and get plenty of exercise.

Let's breathe deeply, reconnect with ourselves
And listen out for any messages our body may give us.
Let's look for signs when we need to rest,
And also for signs of disease or stress.

Let's drop any seeds of shame we might feel about such signs.
And instead, let's talk to experts and ask for help.

Are we bound to doctors' visits? No. We also have the option of engaging in alternative approaches to getting healthier – so that we're working towards getting both our mind *and* our body in the best shape possible for the future.

So, now that we've talked about the relationship that we, as men, tend to have with our bodies from a *health* perspective, I'd like to talk about the relationships we have with our bodies from an image and physical confidence perspective.

EXPLORING OUR RELATIONSHIPS WITH BODY IMAGE

I was watching YouTube the other day and an ad popped up for manscaping. This is normal for me to see, as I'm a millennial man; we're used to the ideas of all sorts of grooming and body curation routines, from moisturizing, tanning and teeth-whitening to beard trimming, shaving and waxing. But it struck me that the older generation may not even know what manscaping is.

Today, we have a relationship with our bodies that previous generations, such as my dad's and grandad's, could never have dreamed of. While they might have secretly longed for a hairier chest, there are now a whole host of new aesthetic ideals placed on men (ones that women have had for generations). The one that we're going to deal with here is that of the size and shape of the body itself – and the impact that societal pressures around different aspects of this have on men's physical and mental health.

MY POINT OF CONNECTION

Scrolling through my phone recently, I found a picture of myself that I had taken in the gym in January. It was one of those 'New Year New You' photos. I didn't like the way my belly was going or how my body was looking, so I had taken the pic to see if I could create change over the next few months.

I had never been confident about my body.

My dad had started me on a fitness regime quite young – combining martial arts, swimming and strength exercises among other things. Yet I was already struggling with my body image by my early teens, with an intense feeling that I didn't look strong or 'manly' enough for someone of my height (I was already over

6 foot by then). And when I saw other people's picture-perfect online videos of home workouts and the like, it made me feel all the worse.

To me, every guy worth his social currency had a buff chest, a six-pack, an athletic build and, as a result, was attractive to the opposite sex. I wanted this attention and adoration. But I didn't have it, as I was the tall, gangly guy with glasses and an awkward personality.

I viewed going to university as an opportunity to change all this and started going to the gym all the time. But the results were always short-lived and my size fluctuated.

In my second year at uni, I was leading a pretty unhealthy lifestyle and put on some weight, so when I went to live in France the following year, I decided to take up running, telling both myself and other people that it was because I wanted to challenge my body and get fitter. Deep down though, I knew it was really more to do with me wanting to lose the weight I had gained and to look better.

In the three months of daily running that followed, I went from 98kg to nearly 75kg. It doesn't take a rocket scientist to tell you that, for a 6' 3" man, that is very light. As a result, I didn't generally feel that great or have a lot of energy, and any injuries that I sustained lasted longer than usual. Ultimately, I was sacrificing my health for aesthetics.

Thankfully, my body perception has changed since then. Daily yoga practice and resistance band exercises now keep me in decent shape. And I am reasonably content with my body.

However, throughout my early twenties, I couldn't help but ask myself questions like:

- *Is it normal for a man of my age to be thinking this way about my body?*
- *Isn't body image something that women are meant to worry about more than men?*
- *Why do I feel so obsessed with the notion of having a sexier, more attractive body?*
- *Why do a lot of men I know seem so secure in their bodies, no matter what shape or size?*
- *Are there ways I can change how I view my body – so that I can feel proud instead of ashamed?*

ANOTHER PERSPECTIVE

My friend Akash Vaghela runs a fitness company (RNT Fitness) that focuses on total life transformation, and is also the author *Transform Your Body, Transform Your Life*, which speaks about mindset and body image.

During a conversation, Akash reminded me that I was by no means alone in my body confidence issues: 'I grew up feeling very insecure about how I looked. I was a "skinny fat" kid. Skinny, but I had *moobs*. It didn't do much for my confidence, but I became obsessed with the topic so started reading up on it.'

Akash never really talked about the issue as he was growing up, as he felt such an inner shame about it. But when his thirst to understand more about fitness and the human body led him to study sports science, he went on to overcome his own negative body image. He did this mainly by shifting from an external motivation, based largely on aesthetics, to a much deeper internal drive, based on really understanding and being able to control, and shape his body with a view to leading a healthier life.

Akash went on to work as a personal trainer in the city for a while before starting his own fitness company, and he was surprised to discover just how many men were struggling with body image in similar ways to he had, but who just didn't have a platform to speak about it.

'Men don't talk about their bodies with other men, if at all. It seems as if there's this whole body image conversation that men just aren't really a part of. Women, on the other hand, tend to have a whole host of conversations around bodies. I think there's a lot to be said for men having these vulnerable conversations – they need to happen more.'

He told me about a client of his who joined one of his RNT Fitness body transformation programmes with the aim of getting a six-pack, but who, along the way, realized that it was his emotional health that needed more of a makeover than his physical appearance.

'Through the physical transformation, my client was able to regain his life … build another business … be a better husband … be a better father. Now that he was taking better care of himself, he could also take better care of them.'

Akash explained that, on the whole, people wouldn't come to him and say, 'I want to improve my anxiety,' or 'I want to improve my mindset.' They would come with an aesthetic goal. But *behind* that, there would often be an emotional reason for them coming. So, they would pour their energy into the physical exercise but really only as an outlet for them to explore the other issues on their own.

'Once you master your body, you have the confidence to master anything,' he says. 'It is essentially the foundation of your life. That's why we hear of people transforming their bodies and then suddenly saying, "I'm going to quit my job and do what I've always dreamed of doing". They feel liberated to do this as they are now taking ownership and direction of their own lives.'

This change of perspective, or mindset, is a lot of what Akash talks about in his book, with the key being that the focus always needs to be in some way about trying to live a better life – giving yourself the opportunity to become the best person you can be – rather than a superficial goal about how *others* perceive you.

ON REFLECTION

Our Body Image Motivations

Thinking back to my experiences in my late teens, it's so weird that there is some kind of unwritten rule about having to go to the gym in order to feel better about yourself. Don't get me wrong, exercise can obviously be a good thing, but it's important that it's for healthy reasons. We often feel under so much pressure to look attractive, manly, sexy or whatever else that we can easily forget that the most important element of fitness is to enhance our health. I definitely wasn't going to the gym for myself when I was in my early twenties – but rather to try to change my body into something that I thought *others* would like more. In fact, I didn't even like going to the gym, and I certainly didn't know what I was doing when I was there!

The Pressure to Conform

On the cover of men's health magazines, there's nearly always a shirtless man who has perfect washboard abs, giving the impression that this is what every man needs in order to feel some level of pride, fulfilment or worth in life. Granted, medically, having less weight around the abdomen is a good thing as it means a lower risk of having any long-term health issues, such as diabetes. But images like this also raise a lot of other matters in my mind …

In July 2020, author and mental health advocate Matt Haig posted on Instagram a screenshot from the *New York Post*'s Twitter page, with the tweet entitled, 'Zac Efron's "Dad bod" transformation on Netflix show shocks fans'. This was in relation to Zac's latest Netflix series called *Down To Earth with Zac Efron* in which he appears bare-chested at one point. The fact that he no longer had the boyish body of his early career seemed to shock people.

Matt's post sparked a discussion on his platform, with people sharing their heartfelt views on men and body image. Many were saying that we will never be happy with our own bodies until we can stop comparisons with others, and many were calling for more holistic and compassionate language around the idea of what a 'healthy body' is.

Matt used this discussion as a chance to talk about what he sees as a key problem around male body image, saying: 'While anorexia is universally seen as unhealthy, gym addiction and kidney-straining protein obsessions can masquerade as healthy while concealing a lot of mental disruption and despair.'

The point he is making here is that, as men, we can become just as obsessed with working out and bulking up as we can about losing weight and getting lean, when, in fact, any obsession taken to an extreme can be potentially unhealthy. According to a 2019 study published in the *International Journal of Eating Disorders*, some 22% of males aged 18–24 who work out to bulk up have what is called 'disordered eating'.

In my mind, there's no question – it's time that we all stopped succumbing so much to societal and media pressure to look certain ways, like the skinny female models or muscular male models that we see in glossy magazines, on social media and in TV shows, like *Love Island,* where people are consistently judged on how they look.

The Ego Trap

During the recent Coronavirus-imposed lockdown, my friends and I set up a daily Zoom workout – our attempt at keeping fit while stuck in our homes – and we managed a solid 60 days before we lost our flame.

Even though my main intention was to feel better in myself and to stay fit while not out and about as much as usual, I started to notice my ego getting in the way: I felt myself wanting to be able to show off my chiselled body on social media.

It was really tempting to bolster my outward image by posting a few pics and using them to draw people to my platform and social feeds. But, I decided against it, because that is not what I want to be about and not what I want my digital imprint to be. I'd rather not be known for something as superficial, and as changeable as how I look, because I want people to feel good about the *stories* that I share.

Knowing Our Why

I recently spoke to Nir Eyal, author and former lecturer in Marketing at Stanford Graduate School of Business and Design. Nir is an advocate of what is called Behavioural Design – a concept that is at the intersection between technology, psychology and business, but which he applies to the processes of habit-forming and decision-making in matters pertaining to health and body image (as well as to matters of technology usage).

In his latest book, *Indistractable: How to Control Your Attention and Choose Your Life*, Nir explores how we can better use our time by being generally less distracted. This, he explains, involves knowing our *why* when it comes to our *habits*, including ones related to our health and body image.

He spoke on my podcast about this in relation to challenges he had with his weight as he grew up, as he was diagnosed clinically obese as a child. 'I remember going to fat camp,' he chuckled, clearly having overcome the worst of it. 'I remember sitting in the doctor's office and being shown a diagram that said: overweight, normal weight, and here's *you*. And it was very much in the red.'

'It was something I had to face in my life: *Why* did I overdo certain things? *Why* did I let food control me? And I'll be honest with you, I wasn't overweight because I was hungry all the time, I was overweight because I was eating my feelings.'

He continued, 'I was overweight because when I was lonely, I would eat. When I was down about myself, I would eat. When I felt bad that I had eaten too much, I would eat. And this is exactly what we see in many people today. It's about fulfilling, or escaping from, some kind of emotion. Whether through food, through exercise, or through another distraction such as social media.'

In coming to this realization, Nir had made a connection between his dietary habits and his mental health. Once he recognized and *understood* this connection (his 'why'), he was able to make the decision as an adult to start redesigning the way he behaved. He would therefore aim to no longer comfort eat in this way and would instead form new habits that would serve his overall health better.

Nir is keen to emphasize just how big an impact this kind of behaviour change can have: 'I like to say that behaviour change is, ultimately, identity change.'

Getting to Know My Own Why

In 2017, when I was 24, I got a personal trainer and put in all of the work I could to give myself a regular fitness routine. I trained four times a week, and planned my meals to make sure I knew where all my food was coming from.

After six months I saw tangible results – a smaller waist and much more muscle definition – but this wasn't why I was doing it (to show off or to reach a certain goal). It was more than this for me. I wanted to know that I could effect change in my body – this amazing vehicle that carries me through each day of life. And I was pleased that, with a positive, focused mindset, and knowledge of my own *why*, that I could!

Now when I go to the gym, I understand what I am going for: to maintain my health and build the body I need to enable me to take on the world. That's it. My whole personality isn't gym-dependent. And I feel no obsessive need to go if ever I'm feeling weak or if it's becoming a chore. Beating ourselves up at the gym, starving ourselves or taking up crazy dieting fads just to be seen as the strongest, most macho person, or whatever, is a flaw in the way we have been socialized to think.

A trick that worked for me when training was keeping a journal in order to check in with the emotional side of what I was doing. There will always be times when you are doing a workout or eating a salad and you think *Why* am I doing this? And there will always be moments where you want to throw in the towel. So, you have to boil everything down to your *why* – so that you can stick at it.

I have taken up the philosophy that I train and eat for *longevity*, not for *superficiality*. And the strength I train for is to have a strong, resilient body for a better chance of good health as I age, rather than to have a beach body! Today, this is my *why*. I take periodic breaks from exercise to check in with myself: *Why* am I doing this again? And if the answer is a vanity-based one, such as wanting a slimmer waist or bigger pecs, I take a step back and reassess my intentions. I take the time to figure out what it is that this could help me with in the long term. Will it make me stronger? Will it make me feel better physically?

It may be worth having a think about what your *why* is, too, as it could change everything for you.

> ### Note to Self
> *I exercise not to look slimmer or sexier,*
> *But to be stronger from the inside out.*
> *If I build a positive and confident mindset,*
> *I can reframe the way I show up for myself.*

A RETURN TO CONNECTION

Seeking Clarity: Knowing What Really Matters

On reflection, it is challenging to look back at my 18-year-old self and be compassionate to the guy who wanted to be the best-looking thing for other people, rather than wanting to make change for my own betterment. When I was sitting in the gym trying to align my goals with what other people thought of me, versus giving my body what it deserved – a fighting chance at a healthy life – I was missing the point of what really mattered.

When I look at the questions that my former lack of body confidence brought up in my mind …

- *Is it normal for a man of my age to be thinking this way about my body?*
- *Isn't body image something that women are meant to worry about more than men?*
- *Why do I feel so obsessed with the notion of having a sexier, more attractive body?*
- *Why do a lot of men I know seem so secure in their bodies, no matter what shape or size?*
- *Are there ways I can change how I view my body – so that I can feel proud instead of ashamed?*

… I now realize that:

- It's perfectly normal for anyone of any age to be aware of and want the best for their own body. It is, after all, the vehicle that carries us through life, so it's good to make sure we look after it the best we can. The key is to aim to ensure that our thoughts about our body are based on what is actually best for *us*, and our health and fitness, rather than what we think will please or get the attention or approval of *other* people.
- Everyone, irrespective of gender, age or anything else, has the right to engage with the notion of body image – and to want to develop their body confidence. It is an outdated notion that only women are concerned with such matters.
- It's only natural to want to feel sexy and attractive to others at times. We all want to feel loved in life. The trick is to remember that confidence, sexiness and attractiveness come as much from the inside as from the outside. So, as much as it's great to get your body in shape, it's more important to develop a healthy, positive mindset.
- Some men may be confident in themselves no matter what shape or size they are as they've got an inner confidence. But there are many other men with just as many hang-ups and insecurities as you, but they just don't show it.

I guess it's best not to make presumptions about how other people might be feeling and instead just openly talk about such things.

- Viewing our bodies as objects that we don't much like is something that many people do, but there are ways around it. One good method is to start reframing how we talk about ourselves, being sure to focus on what we *like* rather than what we *don't* like.

While there will always be room for improvement in how I look,
I appreciate what I am and what I have,
and I'll make these improvements on my own terms, in my own way,
rather than in response to the pressures from others, whether intended or not.

We don't need to do this for other people.
We just need to be the best version of ourselves that we can be.
Let's love our bodies, and love ourselves.

REAL MEN – THE REALITY

It's Time to Drop the Myth That:
Real Men have no worries about their bodies.

It's Time to Remember That:
Real Men take charge of their own health and fitness by learning to appreciate, love, listen to and take care of their bodies. They openly talk about any issues that arise. And they know that a positive body image comes first and foremost from a positive mindset.

CHAPTER 5

REDEFINING SUCCESS
Time to Talk About Self-Worth

We live in times where there seems to be an obsession with the notions of success and failure, as if life is one big exam or race – to see who can be 'the best', the richest, the most powerful, the most famous, or whatever else. And men in particular often seem to feel a certain pressure to achieve, impress, be 'on their game' and come out as 'winners' – with the notion of success seemingly intricately tied with their sense of traditional masculinity.

But who says that life has to follow a pass-or-fail, win-or-lose approach? Isn't it time that we reassess the expectations we carry with us, whether consciously or not, so we no longer spend a large part of our lives feeling inadequate 'failures'? Maybe it's time to redefine what 'success' and 'winning' look like in our own lives, and to re-explore how we deal with perceived failures along the way, so our sense of self-worth is no longer defined by them.

In this chapter, we will look at:

- What the notions of success and failure really mean to us. How do we tend to feel when we view ourselves as failing? Wouldn't it be more helpful to view 'failures' simply as stepping stones to future successes?
- Whether there's space within the idea of success for men to help and support one another, rather than competing with and outdoing one another. Would we not all feel happier in ourselves if there was less focus on toxic competition and more on empathetic collaboration?

Real Man Myth: 'Real Men Never Fail'

REFRAMING 'SUCCESS' AND 'FAILURE'

There's this generally accepted notion in society that people who have a lot of money, a big house, a high-profile job, positive public recognition and other such accolades are the 'success stories' in life. But if that's true, where does that leave the rest of us? Doesn't success sit in more of a grey area – where it's up to us, as *individuals*, to decide what success looks and, more importantly, *feels* like in our own lives? I have had to reassess and redefine what the ideas of both success and failure *really* mean to me many times in my life already – almost always in an attempt to ensure that my sense of self-worth doesn't get caught up with all the superficial ideas of what the media so often portrays as being 'successful'.

MY POINT OF CONNECTION

At school, I was very studious. My GCSE grades were great but during my A-Levels, the pressure got to me. I ended up not getting the grades I had been predicted, and 'failed' to get into my first-choice university.

At uni, I worked hard but ended up graduating with a 2.2, which I felt disappointed with at the time.

And when I went on to do my journalism training, courtesy of a national scholarship, I just about got a merit in my diploma, but never managed to get the desired, and required, 100 words per minute for the shorthand exams.

When I was working at a newspaper and getting into lifestyle feature writing, which is what I had decided I wanted to do, my editor took me aside one day and told me, 'Your writing is just not quite there yet, and it would take a while for us to get it in shape . . . I can see you working in broadcasting, not print. You know, like an arts programme or documentary? I think that's where you're better suited.'

I felt inadequate and ashamed – as if I was a waste of space who didn't belong anywhere. And I started to fall into a spiral of self-doubt, self-pity and imposter syndrome – the latter of which had been growing within me for years.

Thankfully, I was able to pick myself up out of this negative place, with the help of therapy and my supportive family. And I'm now in a good space – running a podcast that I love, writing this book and even running writing-coaching workshops of my own to help people build their confidence, and tell their stories.

However, at the time I couldn't help but ask myself questions such as …

- *What was I doing in any of these courses, or jobs, if I was just going to 'fail' at every turn?*
- *Did I even deserve to be there in the first place?*
- *Why did the feedback from my editor cause me to fall into such a deep spiral of self-loathing and shame?*
- *As a man, shouldn't I feel stronger and be able to deal better with such situations?*
- *Are there ways that I can view such setbacks differently in the future?*

ANOTHER PERSPECTIVE

I had an interesting conversation about the notion of success and self-worth with 29-year-old Abraham (Abe) Adeyemi, a writer and director, who has written and staged numerous plays, and winner of Soho House's global screenwriting competition Script

House in 2019 for his short film *No More Wings* (which also won *Best Narrative Short* at Tribeca Film Festival in 2020).

Abe talked about how so many seeds are often sown during our school years around our own sense of self-worth, based on whether or not we are deemed as a 'success' or 'failure' at this stage of our lives.

'When you're in a grammar school, people are getting straight As,' he said. 'So, even though everyone always used to comment on my academic achievements and my writing in particular, whether it be friends or teachers, I still didn't truly believe that I was really that good.'

'Or maybe I knew it [my writing] was good, but I just didn't think I was excellent enough to have any kind of future success. I didn't feel like I was a standout. I didn't feel like there was anything special about this ability that I supposedly had.'

Abe has gone on to have what most people would view as great success in his writing career, having had numerous projects commissioned for television and seeing *No More Wings* being touted for the BAFTAs, among other awards.

But for him it's never been about external accolades, which, as grateful as he is for them, he has also found to be a bit of a challenge at times – as if being given praise by a particular person, winning a particular award or becoming well known in your field makes you any better at what you do than any of your peers.

For him, it's simply always been about loving what he does. He told me, 'I've just always absolutely adored writing. I've always just loved the words. I remember being in Year Six and being just so excited to do the creative writing SATs paper because I was going to get to write a letter.'

This feeling of excitement and fulfilment about writing and telling stories is something that has stayed with Abe. Knowing that he's spending his days doing something he enjoys and creating something that has the potential to resonate and connect with *other* people, allows him to feel deeply connected to himself and his own creativity.

So, as much as he has achieved on an external level, and I'm sure will continue to achieve, his true happiness comes from communicating and connecting with audiences; by touching the hearts of others in some small way, in turn touches his own heart. This is what success is to him – anything else is a plus.

ON REFLECTION

Failures as Stepping Stones to Success

There are so many things that we can all do in life; each of us has vastly different talents and interests. Yet, often, when something doesn't go quite as we have planned or hoped (in my case my exam and uni results, and my first newspaper job), it's all too easy to take it to heart, let this event take precedence over all else in our mind and start seeing both that *particular* event and *ourselves* as a 'failure'.

I have since realized – with help – that it's crucial to look at the bigger picture and ask ourselves questions like, 'Why did this particular thing not work out? Can I learn from it and go on to do something even better?'

Might it be possible that what I viewed as great failures at the time were never actually 'failures' in the first place? Might it just have been about how I was choosing to *view* them, getting them all wrapped up with my own sense of self-worth? Could these perceived 'failures' actually have been valuable stepping stones to other avenues more suited to me?

Wildly successful TV host and business woman Oprah Winfrey famously once said: 'There is no such thing as failure. Failure is just life trying to move us in another direction.' Former basketball player Michael Jordan (arguably one of the greatest players of all time) once said: 'I have missed more than 9,000 shots in my career. I have lost almost 300 games. On 26 occasions I have been entrusted to take the game-winning shot, and I missed. I have failed over and over and over again in my life. And that is why I succeed.'

Other well-known examples of people who didn't let apparent failures set them back on their journey to doing what they dreamed of doing include inventor Thomas Edison, who patented more than 1,000 items, including the lightbulb, the alkaline storage battery and the phonograph, despite having been told by his teachers that he was 'too stupid to learn anything'; Walt Disney, whose former newspaper editor apparently once told him that he 'lacked imagination and had no good ideas'; and movie mogul Steven Spielberg, who was twice rejected by a school of cinematic arts before going on to make screen classics like *ET*, *Star Wars*, *Schindler's List* and many more.

I recently came across a quote online that resonated with me: 'Never let success get to your head; never let failure get to your heart.' This is a nice simple reminder to essentially never let what we see as 'successes' or 'failures' at different times in our life *define* us, or drag us off course into a rollercoaster of highs and lows. If we can become secure in our own innate self-worth, irrespective of any deemed 'successes' or 'failures', we can find balance and peace of mind.

Do Fame and Wealth Equal Success?

Two things often commonly associated with success are fame and wealth. So, I found a recent newspaper article by ex-professional footballer Marvin Sordell really interesting, in which he shared the story of why he had decided to retire from his lucrative position at the age of just 28.

Martin talked about how he had 'managed to experience some of the greatest highs on offer: playing for England, for Team GB in the Olympics and in the biggest league in the world, the Premier League'; he had scored goals in situations he could only have ever dreamed of as a young boy. By the time he was just 21, he had been signed by a Premier League team for £3 million – a figure which, ridiculously, may not seem like *that* much by footballing standards these days, but which was a huge amount in 2012.

As exciting as it all was, he found the weight of the transfer fee just too heavy to carry. In retrospect, he thinks it was to do with seeking validation from external sources – something that he imagines may be linked to the fact his father hadn't been in his life since he was six. But, whatever the reason, his mental health suffered badly.

At the height of what looked like enormous success on the *outside*, he sunk into a deep depression on the *inside* that, after several months of taking first anti-depressants and then self-medicating through alcohol, culminated in him making an attempt on his own life.

He survived – and even went to football training as normal the day after the suicide attempt without saying a word to anyone about it (both that day and for years to come!) as he felt so deeply ashamed.

Reflecting back on it, he said, 'Where you have a young man with severe confidence issues, low self-esteem, that seeks approval at every turn, and you place them in a high-pressure situation where they are constantly being judged, it probably isn't going to end well.

'What I found at the time, my ego didn't particularly like. I was vulnerable, I was struggling and needed help, but each day I would wake up, put my mask on, and pretend that I was immortal. What I showed the world every day in public was my ego putting up its defence mechanism, to protect it from harm, whereas the real me was withering in private.'

So, while walking away from a dream job may have seemed to many people like a crazy thing to do – and maybe even like a failure at the time – he knew it was, without a doubt, the right decision for him.

Marvin now recognizes that without having gone through all these difficulties, he wouldn't be the self-assured person he is today. And he uses his platform to help spread the message to anyone else struggling with mental health issues that it's OK to go through tough times, that there's no need to feel ashamed, and that it's vital to share how you're feeling with people you love and trust – in order to stop feeling like a failure and to be reminded of your own immense internal strength.

Do Status and Wealth Equal Success?

I recently talked about shifting perceptions of success with 35-year-old Umar Kankiya, a Mental Health Solicitor. Umar represents people detained under the Mental Health Act ('sectioned') who want to appeal their detention and return to life in their communities.

Umar said, 'If you had asked me how I viewed success a few years ago, when I was still working full-time within a law firm, I would have said my ambition was to become a *partner* in a law firm and earn a six-figure sum, on the way to being a judge. But having gone through what I went through with work, it's changed the way I look at things.'

He went on to explain that he would consistently work ridiculously long hours to hit weekly targets, and his bosses would promise him all sorts of financial rewards, but the rewards would just never materialize. 'This cycle [of giving everything for relatively little in return] went on for ten years in total, until I suffered a massive burnout. I was no longer getting enjoyment out of it and it wasn't allowing me to be my true self. So, I ended up leaving.'

Umar had gradually come to the realization that he just didn't want to live this way anymore, and that all the status and money in the world would never be able to make up for the time he had lost out on with his family and for the health issues that he was now suffering as a result of the stress and burnout.

He has recently started a new *part-time*, contracting role, still doing the same type of work but with much more flexible timings. And his view of success looks pretty different now: 'It's about making sure that everything brings me some sort of joy and happiness. As well as being able to help other people, one of the things that I realized was most important to me was being able to have flexibility of work-life balance. I wanted to be able to take my children to school, and be home with my wife. I don't want to be tied to a regime that would threaten that.'

Umar has been so much happier and healthier since he made this change, which just goes to show the utmost importance of getting to know what really matters most to you in life in order to get clear on your own vision of what success looks like for *you*.

Note to Self
At every setback,
I open myself up
To a new version of success.
One that is non-binary.
One that frees me from fixed expectations
And the fear of failing.

RETURN TO CONNECTION

Seeking Clarity: We Are Worthy

Going back to My Point of Connection story on page 163 –
where I explained how I felt I was failing throughout various
stages of school, university and work life – I can now see that, as
unpleasant as it was to feel so bad about myself at the time,
there were valuable lessons to be learned from the
experiences.

So, thinking back to the kind of questions I was asking
myself at the time …

- *What was I doing in any of these courses, or jobs, if I was just going to 'fail' at every turn?*
- *Did I even deserve to be there in the first place?*
- *Why did the feedback from my editor cause me to fall into such a deep spiral of self-loathing and shame?*
- *As a man, shouldn't I feel stronger and be able to deal better with such situations?*
- *Are there ways that I can view such setbacks differently in the future?*

… I now realize that:

- Although I *felt* like I was failing, in truth all that had happened is that I hadn't quite met my *own* randomly set expectations in each of the specific situations. I felt that I had let myself (and a few others) down, which I hated. But this didn't mean that it hadn't been worth me embarking on each of the experiences, as I did, of course, learn a lot from each of them.

- Although I may not have *felt* at the time like I was deserving of the opportunities that I had been given, such as getting my first job as a journalist (my self-worth was pretty much at the bottom of the barrel at the time), I definitely *did* deserve to be there as much as anyone else, as I had worked hard for it and tried my best.

- My sense of self-worth at that time was very much attached to what I could 'achieve' at work and what praise I did (or didn't) get from my colleagues and bosses. It was therefore the sense of failing my editor that led me into a shame spiral.

- We are all just humans, so we all, both men and women, experience setbacks; we all have feelings; and we can all learn to work through these feelings better over time. It's only social conditioning that plants the misguided idea in our head that 'real men' should be 'stronger and able to deal better' with such situations. It's time to dispel such myths once and for all.

- I now know that events like not getting my desired grades or the job I wanted at the paper didn't ever have to be seen as failures in the first place, and instead had the potential to be seen as just minor setbacks, or even as stepping stones to *new* opportunities. The trick is to recognize that it's down to each of us, as *individuals*, to make a choice to view them that way, to not let them interfere with our sense of self-worth, and to move forward with our own firm vision of what success looks, and feels, like in our own lives.

I have to admit that I am still afraid of failure. I don't mean to be, but I am. So, I've decided that the best thing I can do for now is to show myself compassion by ensuring that I try to *learn* from anything I *feel* I have failed at.

It's time to remember that, irrespective of deemed successes or failures in life,
We are, and always have been, worthy of happiness.
Worthy of our own version of success.

Worthy *now*.
Not when we get those grades, that job, that house,
or that money.

Worthy simply because we exist and are trying to be the best we can be.

Let's remind ourselves of this and reclaim our self-worth.

THE ART OF WINNING AT LIFE – TOGETHER!

Having just explored the importance of defining our *own* visions of success and failure, and feeling secure in our sense of self-worth, I'd like to turn to *how* we men tend to feel we have to *be* in order to achieve what we would like in life.

A recent study in the *Harvard Business Review* identified four main masculine norms that tend to define many high-pressure workspaces: show no weakness; strength and stamina; put work first; and dog eat dog.

These 'norms' can start to creep far beyond the workplace if we're not careful, as part of the underlying 'real man myths' web. But do things really have to be like this? Might there be other ways in which we can stride towards the lives we hope for, supporting and reaching out to one another along the way so that we all win *together*, rather than some people winning at the expense of others losing?

MY POINT OF CONNECTION

When I worked for several years as a tabloid journalist, I found myself in a male-dominant culture. In order to get the 'best' story or angle, and to grab the 'hottest' scoop or headline, we often had to ruthlessly compete with one another, which more often than not caused mistrust and interpersonal rifts among colleagues.

Sometimes, such as at celebrity red-carpet events (when I was working for the Entertainment Desk), we literally had to be willing to clamber over one another in a messy cluster in the hope of being the one that the celeb would notice and choose to engage with. Something I never felt quite cut out for.

Another aspect of the work was liaising closely with photographers to capture our stories – something I had thought would be all about helping one another out and having one another's backs. However, that often wasn't my experience.

One particular time, when I was working on my first murder story (which felt like a big deal to me), the photographer that I had been assigned to work with took umbrage against something seemingly innocuous that I did at the start of the day – texted him asking him to come out of a pub so we could urgently follow a new lead.

Instead of just chatting to me about it, accepting my apology or really explaining why he felt that this so undermined him, he spent the rest of the day making things hellish for me – criticizing everything I did, comparing me unfavourably to other junior reporters, cutting me off and speaking over me when we were interacting with the locals – and all because I had asked him in a way that he didn't approve of to leave the pub to support me. To this day, I don't fully understand the dynamic of what was really going on beneath the surface of all this, but I do know that it left me feeling really bad about myself.

This was only one of many experiences where I felt berated and belittled by other men I was working with in journalism. Gone were my hopes of a supportive, collaborative environment in which I would thrive; instead, I found myself in a dog-eat-dog culture where I felt I was never going to quite 'cut it'.

I've since gone on to find a work environment I'm much more suited to, in the form of other styles of writing and podcasting. This work gives me the chance to connect on a more empathetic level with people, share honest stories with them and define my own vision of what success and 'winning' looks like.

But while I was still in the world of journalism, I couldn't help but ask myself questions like ...

- *Do we really need to compete and dominate to be 'successful'?*
- *Why does everyone buy into this culture of having to step on one another?*
- *What's wrong with me that I can't step up to the plate and ruthlessly compete in the way the other guys seem to be doing?*

- *Will leaving the job make me look like even more of a loser to everyone around me?*
- *Is there a way to support each other in life and win collectively, rather than just as individuals?*

ANOTHER PERSPECTIVE

I remember being particularly saddened by a news piece I heard when I was just 21. It was a report on a 58-year-old London-based lawyer who had taken his own life by throwing himself in front of a train on the London Underground. He was a father, husband, partner in a prestigious law firm, and was much admired for his role as a renowned trademark litigator.

Externally, everyone viewed this man as 'winning' in life. People like him – with his status, intelligence, power, influence, wealth, family, respect from others in his industry, etc. – represented everything I thought I wanted to become, so that I, too, could 'win' at life.

But, when it came down to it, he obviously didn't feel like he was winning on the *inside*. What was it that, in spite of all his skills and apparent success, made him feel like this?

Media coverage said that 'he was undergoing a huge amount of stress'. But what was it about this stress that led to him feeling so *very* low and lacking in self-worth? And what was it about our society that meant a man in his position – seemingly so loved and respected by so many – hadn't been able to reach out and ask for help with this stress?

His tragic demise played enormously on my mind.

ON REFLECTION

Winning on the Outside, Losing on the Inside

To help me try to get more insight into the type of things that can lead to a situation like the one just described, I spoke to Ken (not his real name), a 36-year-old former lawyer who had left the fast-paced world of law at a top City firm to start a wellness brand with the aim of providing yoga and fitness to City workers.

Ken had been performing well in his role as a high-powered lawyer, and was very much viewed as a high-flyer by friends, family and colleagues. However, after eight years in the job, he had come to the realization that living under such constant high pressure simply didn't feel like 'winning at life' for him anymore.

While we don't know the full background of the London lawyer who took his own life, it became obvious on discussing the high-pressure corporate world with Ken that there are key things in this environment that can make people feel increasingly disconnected and disenchanted. These include the lack of work–life balance, which can leave you feeling exhausted, empty and unwell; the immense pressure to keep 'achieving', 'dominating' and 'winning' at all costs; and also the huge pressure to keep a *façade* of winning even if you're starting to feel like you're losing inside.

It's all too easy to lose sight of your authentic self and any sense of your innate self-worth when you're playing out this role of what everyone *else* views as successful, as you don't want to let them down or change their perception of you as a strong, hard-working man who wins at life and provides well for the family, etc.

Seeking Guidance and Support
Luckily for Ken, he was able to see a way through all this. Instead of just bottling everything up and keeping it all to *himself* when he started to suffer under the weight of the pressure, he chose to reach out to others, such as by seeking out mentors who could guide and support him. He also chose to observe and *learn* from people who seemed to be managing to find some balance amid all the crazy hours and pressured deadlines. As a result, he set up some healthy non-negotiables for himself, such as exercise on his lunch break and meal prep in advance of work each day so that he didn't skip meals or end up eating junk food.

When Ken finally decided that it was time for him to take the leap out of this world and into his new passion for wellness, he talked about the *fear* he experienced in leaving his job: 'the fear of losing, and not grabbing the outward impacts of winning.'

Yet he knew for sure that he *had* to take the risk, as no promotion or salary could be more attractive or empowering than pursuing his own definition of 'winning at life' – which was to help *others* feel like *they* were 'winning at life', too, by taking charge of their own wellness.

Ken is now happy running his own company. However, he freely admits that he couldn't have got to where he is today if he hadn't gone through the intense experience of working as a City lawyer. As, although it almost broke him at the time, the work gave him a strong sense of both work ethic and drive.

His experience of burnout gave him an increased sense of his own needs and priorities in the end, and a clearer vision for how he wanted his own business to be: less focused on individualistic desires, which give rise to hyper-competitivity, and more focused on giving back to the community – to allow *everyone* he works with, and for, to feel both happy and healthy.

'Winning' on Social Media

Another key area in which there is an unhealthy focus on individualism – and people often not interacting in a supportive way with others – is social media.

Social media is a world filled with content creators who are, in essence, competing with one another for the time and attention of readers, for the highest number of followers, for the highest level of engagement, for sponsorship deals, and the list goes on.

This means people often only portray a very superficial version of themselves on their platforms in order to attract and engage followers. This could be thought of as them portraying only their 'winning' selves – whether looking hot in a new outfit, posing in some glamorous holiday destination, or bending into the 'perfect' yoga pose.

Even during COVID-19, when the majority of people were in government-imposed lockdown, there was a constant stream of overly curated photos, as well as Insta quotes and memes telling people how to 'win' during this time, whether in terms of positive mindset, home-based activities, or whatever else. Constant exposure to posts like these can easily lead to a sense of both inadequacy and envy on the part of viewers – making them feel very much like they're losing at life if their existence feels like a more 'average' one.

As a result, it's easy to find a lot of people tearing each other *down* on social media, rather than building each other *up*, just to try to make themselves feel better (although this is no excuse!). And it can all become rather overwhelming!

I became so overwhelmed and pressurized by social media in all its forms in 2019 that I came off it completely for four months. When I went back on in 2020, I decided after a while that Twitter was no longer a healthy space for me. This is something that a lot of people find weird given that I'm a millennial writer. Personally, I found it to be a platform with so much posturing, implied comparison and other toxic 'noise' on it that I just couldn't see it aligning with how I would like to collaborate, celebrate and support people within my generation and community. I want to show people that we are all learning and in the same boat.

The takeaway here? Simply that it's important to monitor our online activity, just in the same way as our real-life interactions, to ensure that we're not left feeling we're in any way 'losing at life'. It's also important to check that we're not being drawn into any envious, energy-sapping interactions with people who we could simply choose *not* to engage with. Better to try to have more positive, *collaborative* relationships. There's no need to fruitlessly compare ourselves to others or try to show people that we're better or more popular than them – as if life's one big competition. Why not instead look for chances to all help and support each other at 'winning' in life *together*?

Note to Self
Instead of tearing each other down,
Or clambering to be the ultimate winner of life,
I believe that we can win together,
Holding each other up to finish the race.

RETURN TO CONNECTION

Seeking Clarity: Collaboration Over Competition

Thinking back to My Point of Connection stories on page 176, where I shared with you times that I felt belittled by work colleagues, or forced into acting in competitive ways that didn't sit well with me, I can now see that, while these things felt tough at the time, they were key character-building experiences. They allowed me not only to find out more about the professional world of journalism (of which I thought I wanted to be a part), but also to find out about my own values in terms of how I wanted to treat other people – irrespective of what my own individual goals might be.

Returning then to the questions that I found myself posing after my varied experiences working as a journalist …

- *Do we really need to compete and dominate to be 'successful'?*
- *Why does everyone buy into this culture of having to 'clamber over' one another?*
- *What's wrong with me that I can't step up to the plate and ruthlessly compete in the way the other guys seem to be doing?*

- *Will leaving the job make me look like even more of a loser to everyone around me?*
- *Is there a way to support each other in life and win collectively, rather than just as individuals?*

… I now realize that:

- Competition and domination are traditional masculine traits when it comes to the notion of succeeding – just look at the leadership style of many of the world's male political leaders. In my opinion, it's time for a change away from this towards a more collaborative vision of 'success', which doesn't involve the berating of others.

- We live in a society that promotes a strong *fear* of failure. So, in an attempt to *avoid* failing, many people blindly stick to what they know when it comes to 'doing well in life'. Among men, this has traditionally involved one-upmanship and an element of being willing to trample on others. If we want this to change, we need to *be* the change we want to see.

- Although I have felt like a misfit at times for not wanting to continually pit myself against others in an attempt to outdo them, it's important to remember that there is absolutely nothing wrong with me. While some men may feel comfortable with this sort of competition, I just want to do the best I can in my own right without constant comparison to, and rivalry with, others.

- It's up to others what *they* think of me. I decided to choose *myself* and a future for myself that would allow me to start winning on my own terms and helping others to win at life, too.

- If we want to see a shift towards people working *together* more, rather than *against* one another – helping and supporting rather than criticizing and berating, collaborating rather than competing, being compassionate rather than ruthless, lifting each other *up* rather than pulling each other *down* – then we need to think beyond just ourselves and our own needs and wants, to what is best for the greater good, and the wider community.

So, it's time to strip away the notion that we have to win at any cost,
And to instead recognize that winning can be about teamwork and mutual support.

If we create a more inclusive environment in which everyone has an opportunity to 'win', there can be a more cohesive understanding of camaraderie.

Confidence, assertiveness and healthy competition all have their place, but so do humility, kindness and empathy.

And when we are *all* winning at life, rather than just a few among us, we can all experience more love. More belonging. And more connection.

REAL MEN – THE REALITY

It's Time to Drop the Myth That:
Real Men never fail.

It's Time to Remember That:
Real Men recognize that life isn't something to fail or succeed at; life is something to be enjoyed and learned from along the way, with the help and support of the people around you. Real Men have their own subjective vision of what a happy and 'successful' life looks like.

CHAPTER 6

LEARNING TO LOVE COURAGEOUSLY
Time to Talk About Love, Trust and Intimacy

Why is it that so many men, even if we have lots of loved ones around us, don't necessarily feel truly loved and/or don't feel we know how to *give* our love fully and courageously, without holding back? This final chapter explores how, despite *wanting* to experience an all-encompassing love in life, we so often have difficulty being brave enough to open ourselves up to the beauty of love and intimacy in all its forms.

In this chapter, we will look at:

• The sense of love, connection and belonging that friendship can bring to our lives if we learn to build relationships with people who we can really trust and open up to. How can we find these people who we can count on in both good times and bad?

- The importance of learning how to let love into our lives. How can we drop expectations around what we *think* 'love' is meant to look or feel like, and open ourselves to both giving *and* receiving deep, authentic love, trust and intimacy?

Real Man Myth: 'Real Men are Lone Wolves'

VALUING THE GIFT OF FRIENDSHIP

I think it's fair to say that not all friends are created equal. Some might be great at making us laugh, and bringing humour and joy to our life. Some might be great to share particular interests with, whether sports, film, music or whatever else. Some might be great for going out with and socializing. But, as time has gone on, I've realized just how vital it is to also have friends who you can open up to on a more emotional level – people we not only like and have a laugh with, but who we also respect, trust and feel safe with. People who truly see us and know us for who we are at heart. People who accept both our dark side and our light side. rather than just the superficial stuff. So, it's important that we choose our friends wisely.

MY POINT OF CONNECTION

On my return home to London after teaching English for a year on an island in the Indian Ocean – when I was 23 and just about to start my training at the Press Association – I was introduced by a good, old friend of mine to a new group of guys.

My friend knew I was in need of some new connections at the time, as I had fallen out of touch with so many old mates while away at university and then while working abroad.

The new guys seemed great – we got on, had a laugh, exchanged ideas and spent a lot of time together. We would go to the cinema, eat out, go for drinks, celebrate birthdays, and all the other 'normal' stuff friends do . . .

Then, one night, when the five of us were at one of our houses, a conversation came up about sexuality. The unspoken 'alpha male' of the group started saying why he viewed homosexuality as wrong and how no friend of his could ever confide in him that he was gay. I was deeply shocked. Yet I found myself paralysed and staying silent.

None of the other guys said much either, although they seemed to agree with him. And this gave him the space to double down, proclaiming his out-and-out disgust for queer people, at which my shock grew – mixed with confusion, disappointment and anger.

I couldn't believe that people I was spending my time with could think and talk in this terrible way about another group of people. I felt deeply uncomfortable, as I had, and still have, many friends in the LGBT community, and was still getting to grips with my own sexuality at the time.

Yet, almost more horrifying to me was the fact I couldn't bring myself to challenge his homophobia. I felt pathetic about this, but I had a strong sense that if I had spoken up it's unlikely to have ended well – possibly even in a physical fight.

I couldn't even bring myself to leave the house at the time, as I worried it would cause 'too much of a scene'. However, the conversation was the start of me reducing contact with this group of guys and us eventually going our separate ways.

Despite learning from this how important it was to make friends with people who were on the same wavelength as me, and who I could be my true self with, rather than just going along with whatever they were doing and saying, I still made similar mistakes with other new 'friends' in the months and years that followed.

In the years that have passed since then, I have built relationships with people who I can be my honest, authentic self with, and who I can trust to support me no matter what's going on in my life. Many of these good friends I have met through running my podcast.

But at the time, my experiences of trying to connect with new people got me asking myself questions like ...

- Why didn't I speak up against my 'friend's' homophobic outburst?

- *Why was I choosing to spend my time with people who I didn't feel I could be my true self with?*
- *Why do we men often find it so hard to be honest, open and vulnerable with our friends?*
- *What makes a true friend?*
- *How can I have better friends in my life and feel more of a sense of love, belonging and connection among them?*

ANOTHER PERSPECTIVE

Both at the start of the book and in Chapter 3 (page 112) I talked about my friend Nick (Bennett), who started his mental fitness platform Fika after the loss of his best friend Ben to suicide. Nick had been unaware just how much his friend had been struggling through his life, as their conversations hardly ever went further than discussing the trivial, everyday subjects that so many men are most comfortable with.

When it sunk in for Nick that his friend was really gone, it made him think a lot more about the value of true friendship, in particular the friendship between guys. He began to think back over times he and Ben had spent together, asking himself, 'Was Ben OK *then*?' and 'I wonder what he was thinking, or feeling, at that moment?'

He realized that he had never really asked Ben how he was, and had therefore never really been there to listen to his worries. He now wishes so much that he could have connected with him on a deeper level – to let him know that he could trust him, that he loved him, that he was there for him no matter what, and that he would help him in any way he could. But all Nick can do now is learn from this for future relationships and pass the crucial message on to others …

His advice to other men is, 'When you're there with someone, having a pint or whatever, don't just think about the next thing you're going to say. We often think about how we are going to respond, when people sometimes just need us to actively listen.'

Nick doesn't want other men to feel lonely in their friendships anymore, in the way he now realizes that Ben must have been feeling. He stresses the importance of shifting from being emotionally closed off and stilted, to making an effort to be as open, caring and supportive as possible.

'I think about Ben a lot,' he says, 'and it has shown me that we take our friendships for granted. They are such a strength in our life and I don't think we make the most of them because, in a lot of instances, we keep them very surface. And that is the change I want to see.'

ON REFLECTION

The Importance of Emotional Safety

As we've seen, holding a safe space for friends is something that often doesn't seem to be 'the norm' in male friendships. A lot of conversations don't go much past surface level, staying on topics such as sport, music, business, politics, or other topics that we can control the emotional output of.

But, with rising levels of loneliness, mental health issues and suicide, it really is time to make room for more 'real' conversations to happen between friends, and to make sure we have friends with whom we can have these safe, open conversations in the first place.

It's not that every friendship has to be emotionally deep. But it's definitely good to have a think about who would be truly there for you during dark days. If you can't trust that anything you say will be met with the care, love and support it needs, then maybe those people aren't true friends?

Learning to Trust
I spoke to Tony, a 25-year-old engineer, about the role of friendship in his life. He told me that, while he had always felt that he had good mates, when he started to experience anxiety he found himself struggling to trust them to open up to.

'I came to the realization,' Tony said, 'that I didn't feel wholly emotionally safe with them. I didn't think that I could tell them how I was feeling without potential ridicule or shame.' Tony relates this distrust back to not feeling very emotionally safe as a child.

He *wanted* to be able to share his concerns, but just felt he couldn't, partly because of the pressure to be 'a man's man' among his engineer mates, who were pretty traditional in their approach to masculinity.

Gradually though, he began to open up to his girlfriend. He learned from this that it was less scary than he thought to really trust someone. He then started opening up more to his best friend – so that they could start to be more supportive of one another and feel connected on a deeper level.

Tony still finds it hard to open up, but is trying his best. He even joined an online men's group, which has been a game-changer in terms of helping him to grow in confidence when it comes to speaking his own truth.

Finding Your People

Sometimes, as we've just seen in the case of Tony, it might feel too difficult to open up fully to our existing friends. So, it's good to know that support can be found in other places, too – sometimes even in the form of perfect strangers.

I joined a men's support group called *The Mandem* when I was 28, not long after my nana's death. I wasn't sure what to expect at first, but it turned out to be an amazing opportunity to meet new people who had no preconceived opinions about me, no filters. In this space I was able to be heard as my true self, and I ended up making friends with people who really cared.

The premise to a men's support group is simple. A group of perhaps between 8 and 12 men meet up regularly and maybe watch a film that touches on the topic of masculinity before having a discussion about it, with the option to share how they feel about things happening in their own lives, too.

One particular group that inspires me is MenSpeak, founded by my friend Kenny Marmarella D'Cruz, whose incredible story appears in Chapter 2 (see page 77). MenSpeak offers space for men both to open up emotionally and to challenge the toxic impact that traditional, outdated notions of masculinity can often have on us without us even realizing.

Kenny has been running groups like this for over two decades. He offers a mix of check-in sessions, open groups, and closed groups (where the same group of guys meet regularly over a long period). But no matter which group you join, Kenny says it's about 'cutting the crap and being honest'.

No-one has to share anything they don't want to, of course. But he wants there to be authenticity in each conversation: 'One of the ground rules is: play big enough to get it wrong. Don't play small and be a good actor and try to be liked. It's not about being liked. It's about getting real.'

'It's a challenging space. But a good kind of challenging,' he says. 'In the closed groups, a lot of the men have been together for years. They know each other, they care for each other. They will know what the other person in the group is avoiding or what needs celebrating, or what needs to be asked about that might have been glossed over. They will know not to go for the kill, because it's not about the kill; it's about *how we can be safe together*, open up and allow things to pass so that we can step into our power.'

'For me, it's about holding a space and asking the right questions so the men uncover their truth for themselves,' says Kenny. His work has now supported thousands of men worldwide, with groups both in London and online. He has also created a training programme for men who want to run their own groups.

Supporting Friends in Need

As much as I have spoken about the importance of having friends who will be there for you in your times of need, it's also important to be there for *your* friends in return – even if this involves you stepping outside of your normal comfort zones.

I learned this the hard way when, in April 2020, deep in the lockdown brought on by the Coronavirus pandemic, a childhood friend tagged me in a Facebook video of him. He was heading on foot and, according to him, armed, towards the nearest hospital to 'fight the zombies associated with the virus before it spread across our borough in northwest London'.

I knew my friend had had mental health issues in the past and had been sectioned a few years before, but this was the first time I was seeing a schizophrenic delusion for myself. It was frightening to see him in this state, and to think about what might happen if the authorities approached him.

Some friends and I spent the evening trying to reach him, piecing together what we knew about his condition, and reaching out to local mental health services for help.

Fortunately, nothing further came of the situation; he ended up returning home once the delusions had subsided, before ever reaching the hospital.

To my shame, I've realized as I write this book that I haven't spoken to him about the incident, or his general mental health, in the months since. I have found myself not knowing how to reach out or what to say. This is largely out of fear of saying something that might set him back, but also, if I'm completely honest, out of a sense of pure discomfort with the situation.

I do plan to reach out to my old friend soon to see how he is doing. It's crucial that I do what I'm encouraging others to do and really make 'time to talk', no matter how difficult that may feel. In the meantime, I have started looking into Mental Health First Aid courses that could give me a better understanding of what to do if people like him, or other friends, need mental health support in the future.

Celebrating Life

So far we have talked about how having a loving, engaged network of friends can help us get through the toughest of times. But friendship doesn't just have value in *tough* times, of course. It's also about creating beautiful new memories together – sharing, laughing and celebrating life together!

When a group of my good friends meet up, it makes me feel so happy. Equally, meeting with friends one-on-one, to catch up on where they're at in life, is one of the most important things to me.

The time I spent with a close friend in Belgium a few months before my nana's death, when we had just found out how ill she was, was enlightening; it showed that true friendship can help you feel heard, happy, connected and loved, even during the most difficult times in life. Then when my nana passed away, I went to Holland with some of my closest friends. We ate loads, talked, laughed and generally enjoyed being together in another country – and the sense of love and belonging helped me to heal.

It's so important to take the time to treasure friendship and let our friends know just how much they mean to us and just how much we love them.

> ## Note to Self
> *I deserve to be supported and heard.*
> *I deserve to not feel alone.*
> *It is important to have friends*
> *Who can help me weather the storms of life.*

RETURN TO CONNECTION

Seeking Clarity: We Are Not Alone

Thinking back now to My Point of Connection experience(s) on page 191, when I felt unable to speak up against the homophobic opinions that I so strongly disagreed with and when I felt such a need to just fit in, it makes me sad to remember how lost and disconnected I felt at that point in my life. I no longer have space in my life for such inauthentic experiences in my friendships.

Thinking back to the kind of questions I was asking myself at that time …

> - *Why didn't I speak up against my 'friend's' homophobic outburst?*
> - *Why was I choosing to spend my time with people who I didn't feel I could be my true self with?*

> - *Why do we men often find it so hard to be honest, open and vulnerable with our friends?*
> - *What makes a true friend?*
> - *How can I have better friends in my life and feel more of a sense of love, belonging and connection among them?*

... I now realize that:

- I didn't speak up against my friend's outburst as I didn't feel emotionally safe enough (or even physically safe enough in this instance) to speak up as my true self. My silence was driven by fear – fear of not fitting in, fear of rejection, fear of being left on my own. I can see now that I was stuck in a pattern of trying to please *other* people rather than simply being true to myself; I was feeling lost and therefore craving a sense of belonging and connection anywhere I could get it.

- I chose to spend time with these guys as I didn't yet properly know or love myself, which meant I was desperately searching for myself in others. I let these guys choose me as a friend based on the confident, outgoing, thick-skinned image that I was presenting to the world, rather than based on my true, sensitive self with whom I wasn't yet comfortable.

- As we've repeatedly seen in this book, men seem to find it difficult to be honest, open and vulnerable mainly out of fear of looking weak and 'unmanly'. Because of the traditional notions of how men are *supposed* to act around one another (strong, self-sufficient, etc.), it often doesn't feel like there's room for emotional honesty and depth without an element of embarrassment or shame. It's time for this to change. To this end, it's so important to have a wide variety of friends – different genders, ages, backgrounds, life experiences – who all bring different things to the table, including some who bring complete emotional safety.

- As I have grown into myself, I've realized that I want to find friends with whom I can be my authentic and honest self, even if we have different views. People with whom there is no need for bravado or pretence. People I feel safe to share my deepest worries and problems with. People I can count on to hold me up in times of trouble. And people who I accept, love and hold space for in return. To me, a *true* friend is someone who can meet you where you are at – where you can both be supported to be the best person you can be. Someone who brings a deeper level of trust, security, authenticity, love, belonging and connection to your life.

- The first step in ensuring you have a loving group of friends is to make sure you really know and feel comfortable with yourself and your own values *first* – so that you can then show up for your friends by simply being who you are – not perfect, just true. I feel very grateful that I now have a set of friends who give me such a strong sense of emotional safety. Space is held for me when I need it – as well as me holding space for them when they need it. In this way, we all get to experience a deep sense of love, belonging and connection in our relationships. We are there to hold each other up as we go through life's ebbs and flows. We are there to support each other (not drain each other of energy), to cheer one another on (not knock one another down), to pick each other up when we fall (without embarrassment or shame).

Be courageous.
Be you. Be me.
Continually be there for one another.

Be present and make sure you are listening,
As well as talking;
Give love and support,
As well as being open to receive love and support.

Strong friendships can be a game changer in life,
Allowing us to feel truly loved,
And to show up as our best self in the world.
Let's really value our friendships,
And let our friends know how much we love and value them.

LETTING LOVE IN

In Chapter 2, we talked about learning to love our authentic selves – which I've come to realize is the basis for letting all other forms of love into our lives. We've just talked above about the depth of love, connection and belonging that *friendship* can bring to our lives. And I've touched on *familial* love here and there throughout the book. Now, I'd like to talk about love between romantic partners. How do we view and show up for this, as men? Do we have false expectations about what it looks like? And do we struggle with the trust and intimacy required to let it fully into our lives?

MY POINT OF CONNECTION
I have not yet been in love.

As a teenager, love was captivating to me. I got to know it through films like Brown Sugar, Love Actually, About Time *and* The Notebook. *I binged on a diet of R'n'B and Reggae love ballads. And most books I read were centred round some sort of relationship (at 17, I thougt* The Time Traveller's Wife *might be the best love story I would ever encounter).*

As I grew up, the romantic image of love and intimacy I had encountered in such films, music and books didn't become a reality for me.

I kissed my first girl at 16, during a game of spin the bottle (the age at which most of my guy friends were losing their virginity). While most guys were focused on sex and having a trawl of girls on their arm, I was shy and more interested in developing a connection with people. But I found it hard to find that emotional connection so didn't date much.

I went to prom with someone I liked, but we were just good friends. I went speed dating when I was 22, but left with new friends rather than a partner. And still, now, at 29, I haven't been in any significant long-term relationships. Don't get me wrong, I've had a few romantic explorations along the way, but nothing that has gone very far, and I've never introduced any partners to my parents. In 2020, thanks to COVID-19, my plans to 'date more this year' went out the window.

A year or so ago, a conversation about relationships came up with my dad one evening, as we were building a new bed for my younger sister. Presumably feeling concerned on some level that I had never shared much about that aspect of my life to him and my mum, he asked me if I thought a lot about dating.

Feeling like an embarrassed teenager, I shrugged my shoulders. Of course I think about dating! But I found myself simply not knowing what to say about it to my dad, and felt really uncomfortable. He went on to suggest that the way to get more dates and find love was to be 'cocky', 'bold', 'confident' and 'loud'. All traits that I'm pretty sure helped my dad secure the attention of my mum in the '90s. But all of which, I simply am not.

I responded, 'So I can't just be myself?'

This time it was my dad's turn to shrug, as he responded, 'Up to you.'

We got on with building the bed, but I was left with an acute feeling that I just don't get what love really means, or how to let it into my life. Maybe I wasn't confident or 'manly' enough to attract partners.

I never seem to be able to make space for love. I find myself sort of hoping that someone will just come along out of nowhere, like a thunderbolt, and show me what it is.

I can't help but ask myself questions like ...

- Isn't love something that should feel natural and easy to find and experience?
- Have I not experienced true love yet because there is something lacking in me?
- Are unrealistic expectations around love holding me back?
- How can I get better at letting love into my life?
- Will I ever find love?

ANOTHER PERSPECTIVE

I recently spoke to a 30-year-old man called Oliver, who was mugged and stabbed one night during his second year at university, when he was 20.

Up until then, Oliver had been pretty laid-back about life, a guy who never got too fazed by things. But the attack left him struggling with intrusive, negative and even suicidal thoughts, which he felt he had no-one to talk to about.

He ended up dropping out of university and moving to London for work. But his negative thoughts and feelings continued, to the point that he made an attempt on his own life.

It was only after his suicide attempt that Oliver started talking to people about what he had been going through. He sought professional help in the form of therapy, was diagnosed with PTSD (post-traumatic stress disorder) and depression, and was prescribed medication to help him through.

Despite making significant progress, Oliver ended up relapsing the following year when he came off his medication too quickly, which resulted in him making another attempt on his life while in a relationship with someone.

He hadn't told his girlfriend the full reality of his situation, so the whole thing came as a huge shock to her and they ended up parting ways. Oliver also realized that not sharing his full truth with her had been a huge burden on him, as well; it had made him feel both acutely lonely and inauthentic while in the relationship.

He therefore made the decision that he would no longer hide the truth of his PTSD from potential partners. He would, instead, be brave and honest about his 'baggage', as he puts it, from the very outset. So anyone who wasn't comfortable with it, or didn't feel strong enough in themselves to deal with it, would have the option to walk away from the very first date onwards.

Oliver realized that only by being 100% himself in this way – ready for both the good *and* bad to be embraced – would he create a firm foundation of authenticity and trust on which love could potentially grow. And only by relieving himself of the burden of carrying his worries *alone* would he create a space into which true love might just enter.

This was a new way for him to think – recognizing that he was fully *deserving* of love despite the emotional and mental health issues he had experienced. There was nothing to hide or be afraid of; the right person would love him for his *entire* being.

At the time of writing, Oliver was still very much enjoying dating – ready to meet each person with love and openness, in celebration of life.

ON REFLECTION

Opening Ourselves to Love

As we've explored before in the pages of this book, laying your cards on the table is something that many men are brought up believing that they simply shouldn't do. Being too open, soft and vulnerable, is a sure way to have people view you as weak and lose interest in you, right? But, what if, as Oliver came to believe, this is actually the *only* way to start building a strong foundation for true love?

One definition of the cultivation of love is that by renowned author and research professor Brené Brown, who has spent the past two decades studying courage, vulnerability, shame and empathy. Brené says love will grow 'when we allow our most vulnerable and powerful selves to be deeply seen and known, and when we honour the spiritual connection that grows from that offering with trust, respect, kindness, and affection'.

So, maybe instead of chasing a superficial notion of what we *think* love is meant to look like – all hearts, stars and happy-ever-afters like in books and films – we just have to be brave enough to strip things back and be honest and authentic.

Breaking Down Misconceptions of Love

David McQueen, a 52-year-old executive leadership coach, spoke on my podcast about how he built the foundations of love with his wife of 25 years, Madeline, with whom he has two adult daughters. And not only do he and his wife live together, they work together, which can only go smoothly when the relationship is super strong.

'We're best friends,' David said. 'When we first started going out, we were in different cities, so we *talked* a lot about *everything*.

This means that our relationship isn't fragile. It's quite deep because we understand each other and communicate a lot.'

'I think in many ways with a lot of the projected personas on social media and reality TV, people are trying to live up to things that aren't real. If there was one bit of advice I could give to couples, it would be not to confuse love with marriage. Some people think love will come by virtue of marriage, but that isn't the case.'

'I think the other advice would be to be aware of the kind of Disney, or Hollywood, lie, that when you meet someone, suddenly all the birds start singing and you will live happily ever after. It just doesn't work like that.'

He added, 'Some of it's about recognizing that you're going to have to do work on yourself, as well as on your relationship, which is hard you know … The challenge is loving yourself first. And not having expectations of the other person that you're not willing to ask of yourself first.'

'I believe love is always there,' he said. 'But I also think that there needs to be an honest conversation about the fact that it's hard work.'

Becoming the Person We Want to Be in Love
I also spoke about love and relationships with 37-year-old life coach and public speaker Sope Agbelusi. Sope met his wife-to-be while at university, and they had started their

family by the time he was 22. So, he had to mature quickly to become the person he wanted to be for them.

His friends at the time were, on the whole, acting like many guys of that age do: concerned with 'the number of girls they could get' – essentially physical conquests. That wasn't really his thing as he viewed a lasting, loving relationship like that of his parents more as the pinnacle of love, yet he had been playing along all the same.

'So, when I met my wife-to-be, I wasn't very committed to the relationship. I was one foot in and one foot out, with a lot of distractions around me. But Shirene quite rightly called me out on this. So I had to think about what I wanted from a relationship and why: "Was I willing to open up to, and commit to, a relationship with someone who I could potentially see myself spending the rest of my life with, or, was I willing to pass that up for the chase of physical attraction and the unknown?"'

He chose the first of the two options and they subsequently both 'had to work together to heal from previous romantic relationships. I had to unlearn toxic behaviours and I began to look at the world differently.

'My wife had to learn to open up to me, and I had to learn to open up to her, and while that was not seen as the done thing for a lot of men in relationships, it was something we felt was necessary for the success of ours. I think it's why we have made it so far.

'We spent hours together just talking, laughing, watching stuff, getting to know one another and challenging one another in both good and bad ways. And through this, our emotional connection grew stronger and stronger. With her, I could now be open. I could be vulnerable. I could be real. I could be myself, both the good and the bad – and vice versa.

'I had to learn that love does not miraculously appear in a relationship; it is something that comes from the other person wanting the best out of their partner and both helping and allowing them to get there.

'You never know what love is until you experience it. A lot of people have lots of theoretical expectations around love. But, as far as I can tell, love for me is going to be different from what love is for you.'

It's up to each of us to bravely find our own path.

Note to Self
Being courageous in love
Starts with knowing I deserve it,
Knowing that I am worthy of connection,
And being willing to trust, open up and surrender to it.

A RETURN TO CONNECTION

Seeking Clarity: We Are Love

Looking again now at my Point of Connection story in light of my conversations with Oliver, David and Sope among others, I can see that the question I asked my dad about what it takes to find love – 'So I can't just be myself?' – was an instinctively good one.

Ultimately, only if you know, love and can be your true self with another person – and only if that person accepts and loves you for *all* that entails – will you really be able to experience the true power of all-encompassing love.

Thinking about the questions I asked myself above …

- *Isn't love something that should feel easy and natural to find and experience?*
- *Have I not experienced true love yet because there is something lacking in me?*
- *Are unrealistic expectations around love holding me back?*
- *How can I get better at letting love into my life?*
- *Will I ever find love?*

… I now believe that:

- Love and relationships can indeed come about naturally when you meet the right person at the right time. They're just not necessarily easy to maintain, as it takes trust, effort and patience to nurture lasting, healthy, loving relationships.
- Just because I haven't yet experienced true love does *not* mean there is something wrong with *me*. It simply comes to us all at different times in life. However, I realize that I do find it hard to let my guard down and fully trust people, which means it is more difficult for me to engage in full-on love and intimacy, whether emotional or physical. This is temporary though, not forever.
- It's important for us *all*, myself included, to recognize and drop any unrealistic expectations of love that may be holding us back from seeing the true love that can blossom from emotional connection. It would be useful for me to work on releasing the subconscious notions I picked up from books and films that love is full of romantic gestures, feel-good vibes and shiny happy-ever-afters. It's up to anyone in search of love to get real, be true to ourselves and our partners, accept the bad with the good, and be willing to work through any challenges that come up along the way.
- To get better at letting love in, we all have to get better at first feeling comfortable with and truly loving ourselves;

only then can we truly open our hearts and souls to others. Until now, I have been on a journey of learning about, trusting and loving myself more, so haven't been quite ready to open my heart to the fullness of true love in my life.

• Although at the time of writing this, I still hadn't experienced love in the way I would like, it is most definitely something I believe I will find. Or maybe it will find *me* once I'm ready.

Loving ourselves has to be the first focus,
If we want to experience deep love in our lives.

There's nothing weak or 'unmanly' about trusting and opening up to our partners,
Being emotionally vulnerable, honest and intimate,
Openheartedly giving and receiving.

Talking and listening to them are courage in action –
So that we live from a place of sharing and togetherness
Rather than loneliness and separation ...

All of which connects us.
All of which leads us to love.
All of which leads us to the sense of true belonging that we long for and deserve.

REAL MEN – THE REALITY

It's Time to Drop the Myth That:
Real Men are lone wolves.

It's Time to Remember That:
Real Men, and *all* genders, need love and support from others to feel connected, to feel a sense of belonging and to thrive. While love will be different for different people, we are *all* deserving of, and capable of experiencing it. We just need to open ourselves fully and courageously to it; commit our time and energy to it; and not be limited in our perceptions of what we feel it 'should' be; instead, embracing whatever beautiful form it comes along in.

A FINAL NOTE

My hope is that you will have found at least *some* seeds of insight in the stories and ideas that I've shared in this book, and that the topics covered can serve as useful conversation starters about issues that really matter.

We can no longer claim to be surprised when we hear the scary stats about men feeling lonely, suffering from mental health issues and suicide rates, which are the result of years of men being discouraged from expressing themselves. This isn't to say that chemical imbalances aren't real – they most definitely are – but sometimes it can be our own self-limiting beliefs, actions or *lack* of certain actions that fuel these negative emotions and hinder change.

It's time to break free from the old binds, time to challenge our own prejudices – our ideas of what we've been told it means to be 'real men'. It is time to drop the myths, accept new possibilities and embrace new realities.

It's time for a new phase of masculinity, one which …

- Rejects toxic 'shoulds', debunks the one-size-fits-all 'real man' myths and drops inauthentic masks
- Sees strength in openness, diversity, vulnerability and authenticity
- Normalizes asking for help
- Starts mental health conversations
- Recognizes and respects *us* – whoever we are, wherever we come from, wherever we're going.

Let's start talking.

And let's put love, belonging and connection at the heart of these conversations, because striving for these things, above all else, is what will allow us to live the best life we can.

Life is worth living. Life is worth fighting for. It's time to talk.

FURTHER READING
Books That Moved Me

I have read a lot of books that have kept me company and supported me over the past few years, particularly on days when I have felt lonely, disconnected or lacking in love and any sense of belonging. Without these books, I am unsure if *this* book would have come into being. Below is a selection of my most favourite reads for you to consider and maybe draw from. I hope that, if you choose to read any of them, they give you as much comfort, reassurance and inspiration as they have me.

USEFUL MENTAL
HEALTH RESOURCES

Your local doctor or health service is a good first port of call if
ever you feel unwell, distressed, in despair or in need of help.
But below is a list of other potential resources for mental
health information, support and guidance, depending on
where you're based. Although by no means exhaustive, I hope
it's a useful starting point. Many of the charities cater for
emergency calls.

CHARITIES

Befrienders Worldwide – www.befrienders.org
Beyond Blue (Australia) – www.beyondblue.org.au
Campaign Against Living Miserably (CALM; UK) – www
.thecalmzone.net
Crisis Services Canada (Canada) –
www.crisisservicescanada.ca/en
Crisis Text Line (Canada, Ireland, UK, US) –
www.crisistextline.org

It's OK to Talk (India) – www.itsoktotalk.in
Mind (UK) – www.mind.org.uk
Samaritans (UK) – www.samaritans.org
Shaw Mind Foundation (UK) – www.shawmind.org
The Trevor Project (US) – www.thetrevorproject.org

FINDING A THERAPIST
Better Help (US) – www.betterhelp.com
Black and Asian Therapy Network (UK) – www.BAATN.org.uk
Black Minds Matter (UK) – www.blackmindsmatteruk.com
British Association of Counsellors and Psychotherapists (UK) –
    www.bacp.co.uk
Frontline Therapist (UK) – www.frontlinetherapist.com
Talkspace (US) – www.talkspace.com

WELLNESS PLATFORMS
A CALL TO MEN – www.acalltomen.org
*On a campaign to create a world where all men and boys are
    loving and respectful, and all women and girls are valued and
    safe.*

Manual – www.manual.co/about
*Challenging the outdated notion that real men shrug their
    shoulders and carry on; instead, empowering them with*

all the information they need to proactively own their
wellbeing.

Human Aspect – www.thehumanaspect.com
Offering a 'Life Experience Library' of videos to make sure no-one
ever feels alone with their challenges; it is easier to overcome
your challenges if you can hear from someone who has already
done so.

Fika – www.fika.community
On a mission to make Mental Fitness mainstream – to improve
our core skills, reduce the risk of mental health decline and help
us all to flourish.

MenSpeak Men's Group – www.mensgroups.co.uk
Confidential spaces for men to hang out, drop facades, be heard
and get real – in order to get more out of life.

ACKNOWLEDGEMENTS

We are but a sum of our memories in the end. This book has been a reminder of this, in that I am filled with a multitude of memories. And I am grateful for every single one.

As memories – and stories – make this book, so do people.

To my amazing editor Kelly Thompson – you have gone above and beyond to get the best out of me, pulling my voice centre stage when I tried to hide, and reassuring me at every meltdown. Editing with care, consideration and plenty of capital letters, Kelly, you really talked me off a few cliffs. The book is immensely better for it, and I am eternally grateful. Thank you!

To my formidable agent Natalie Jerome – thank you for seeing something in me even when I don't see it myself. You fought for this book. You believed in this book. You gave me space and time to talk. You listened to me. You are a dream.

To Jo Lal and the rest of the team at Welbeck Balance – thank you for taking a chance on me, believing in my writing, and helping to shape the vision of the book.

To Clarissa – this book would not exist without the force that is you. You first encouraged me to create the podcast that would go on to become 'Time to Talk'. Thank you for supporting me. You are a visionary and believed in me when I didn't believe in myself.

To Raifa and Derek – I can't thank you guys enough for saying 'yes' when we braved the world of podcasting together. Thank you for having been so instrumental in my life journey.

To the people whose stories and voices are in the book, whether real names are given or not – I could not have done this without your willingness to talk so openly and honestly with me both on and off the podcast. Thank you, each and every single one of you, for your immense courage and generosity. I am immensely grateful for all your contributions.

To my best men Dillan, Sam, Eden, Nathaniel, Richie, Sope, Nic, Omar, Errin, Aramide, Ashley and Phil – an enormous thanks for holding me at the various points when I felt I had no more to give; throwing water on my face when I couldn't get up in the morning; showing me that everything has an upside; making me laugh when I most needed it; and providing a shoulder to cry on when I was out of all other options.

To all of my friends along the way – your names are too numerous to mention. Know I love you and that your input into my life doesn't go unnoticed or unappreciated.

Last but not least, this book would mean nothing if it weren't for my big, loving family – with so many aunties, uncles, cousins, godparents and more. I'd like to extend a huge heartfelt thanks to all of them, including …

My sister, who will send me a text at 3am to say 'I love you x'.

To all my cousins, who are also my friends – you support me through my dramas.

To my beautiful nieces – you remind me of the importance of being a wholehearted man.

To my nephews, Theo, Gabriel, and my adopted nephew Zion – this is a book for you to read as you grow into men; a place to learn that it's not only OK to be open, honest and vulnerable, but that it will, in fact, make you a stronger, braver and more authentic man in the end.

To my aunties and uncles, who have watched me stumble and stutter when trying to explain the book.

To Mum, who worried if I was eating, resting and hydrating enough as I wrote this.

To Dad, who made me laugh to forget about how much pressure I was putting on myself to deliver.

To both my parents – I could not have got this book finished without you. I love you to the moon and back.

And finally, to my grandparents. Three gone, and one surviving. I hope that I am making you proud – proud that you made the journey of tens of thousands of miles from the hills of Jamaica to the rocky shores of England. Thank you for making that journey and laying the foundations for my story.

TriggerHub.org is one of the most elite and scientifically proven forms of mental health intervention

Trigger Publishing is the leading independent mental health and wellbeing publisher in the UK and US. Clinical and scientific research conducted by assistant professor Dr Kristin Kosyluk and her highly acclaimed team in the Department of Mental Health Law & Policy at the University of South Florida (USF), as well as complementary research by her peers across the US, has independently verified the power of lived experience as a core component in achieving mental health prosperity. Specifically, the lived experiences contained within our bibliotherapeutic books are intrinsic elements in reducing stigma, making those with poor mental health feel less alone, providing the privacy they need to heal, ensuring they know the essential steps to kick-start their own journeys to recovery, and providing hope and inspiration when they need it most.

Delivered through TriggerHub, our unique online portal and accompanying smartphone app, we make our library of bibliotherapeutic titles and other vital resources accessible to individuals and organizations anywhere, at any time and with complete privacy, a crucial element of recovery. As such, TriggerHub is the primary recommendation across the UK and US for the delivery of lived experiences.

At Trigger Publishing and TriggerHub, we proudly lead the way in making the unseen become seen. We are dedicated to humanizing mental health, breaking stigma and challenging outdated societal values to create real action and impact. Find out more about our world-leading work with lived experience and bibliotherapy via triggerhub.org, or by joining us on:

🐦 @triggerhub_

f @triggerhub.org

📷 @triggerhub_

Printed in the USA
CPSIA information can be obtained
at www.ICGtesting.com
JSHW031710140824
68134JS00038B/3631